ARTHUR MILLER

All My Sons

with commentary and notes by
TOBY ZINMAN

Series Editor: Enoch Brater

Bloomsbury Methuen Drama
An imprint of Bloomsbury Publishing Plc

B L O O M S B U R Y
LONDON · NEW DELHI · NEW YORK · SYDNEY

Bloomsbury Methuen Drama

An imprint of Bloomsbury Publishing Plc

Imprint previously known as Methuen Drama

50 Bedford Square	1385 Broadway
London	New York
WC1B 3DP	NY 10018
UK	USA

www.bloomsbury.com

**BLOOMSBURY, METHUEN DRAMA and
the Diana logo are trademarks of Bloomsbury Publishing Plc**

This edition first published 2010
Reprinted 2012 (three times), 2013 (twice), 2014, 2015

British Library Cataloguing-in-Publication Data
A catalogue record for this book is available from the British Library.

ISBN: PB: 978-1-4081-0838-3
ePDF: 978-1-4742-2561-8
ePUB: 978-1-4742-2560-1

Library of Congress Cataloging-in-Publication Data
A catalog record for this book is available from the Library of Congress.

Series: Student Editions

Printed and bound in India

Contents

Arthur Miller: 1915–2005

1915   17 October: Arthur Asher Miller born in New York City,
the second of Isidore (Izzy) and Augusta (Gussie) Barnett
Miller's three children. His brother Kermit born in 1912,
sister Joan 1922.

1920–   Attends PS 24 in Harlem, then an upper-middle-
28   class Jewish neighbourhood, where his mother went to
the same school. The family lives in an apartment
overlooking Central Park on the top floor of a six-storey
building at 45 West 110th Street, between Lenox and Fifth
Avenues. Takes piano lessons, goes to Hebrew school and
ice-skates in the park. His Barnett grandparents are
nearby on West 118th Street. In summers the extended
family rents a bungalow in Far Rockaway. Sees his first
play in 1923, a melodrama at the Schubert Theatre.

1928   His father's successful manufacturing business in the
Garment District, the Miltex Coat and Suit Company,
with as many as 800 workers, begins to see hard times
faced with the looming Depression. The family moves
from Manhattan to rural Brooklyn, where they live at
1350 East 3rd Street, near Avenue M, in the same
neighbourhood as his mother's two sisters, Annie
Newman and Esther Balsam. Miller plants a pear tree in
the backyard ('All I knew was cousins'). Celebrates his
bar-mitzvah at the Avenue M Temple.

1930   Transfers from James Madison High School where he is
reassigned to the newly built Abraham Lincoln High
School on Ocean Parkway. Plays in the football team and
injures his leg in a serious accident that will later excuse
him from active military service. Academic record
unimpressive, and he fails geometry twice.

1931   Early-morning delivery boy for a local bakery before
going off to school; forced to stop when his bicycle is
stolen. Works for his father during the summer vacation.

1933   Graduates from Abraham Lincoln High School and
registers for night school at City College. He leaves after
two weeks ('I just couldn't stay awake').

1933–   Earns $15 a week as a clerk for Chadwick-
34   Delamater, an automobile-parts warehouse in a run-

down section of Manhattan that will later become the site for the Lincoln Center for the Performing Arts. He is the only Jewish employee, and experiences virulent anti-Semitism for the first time.

1934   Writes to the Dean of the University of Michigan to appeal against his second rejection and says he has become a 'much more serious fellow' ('I still can't believe they let me in'). Travels by bus to Ann Arbor for the autumn semester, with plans to study journalism because 'Michigan was one of the few places that took writing seriously'. Lives in a rooming house on South Division Street and joins the *Michigan Daily* as reporter and night editor; takes a non-speaking part in a student production of Shakespeare's *King Henry VIII*. Moves to an attic room at 411 North State Street and works part-time in an off-campus laboratory feeding past-prime vegetables to thousands of mice.

1936   Writes his first play, *No Villain*, in six days during semester break and receives a Hopwood Award in Drama for $250 using the pseudonym 'Beyoum'. Changes his major to English.

1937   Enrols in Professor Kenneth T. Rowe's playwriting class. Rewrites *No Villain* as *They Too Arise* and receives a major award of $1,250 from the Theatre Guild's Bureau of New Plays (Thomas Lanier – later Tennessee – Williams was another winner in the same competition). *They Too Arise* is produced by the B'nai Brith Hillel Players in Detroit and at the Lydia Mendelssohn Theatre in Ann Arbor. Receives a second Hopwood Award for *Honors at Dawn* when Susan Glaspell is one of the judges. Contributes to *The Gargoyle*, the student humour magazine. Drives his college friend Ralph Neaphus east to join the Abraham Lincoln Brigade in the Spanish Civil War, but decides not to go with him. Months later Neaphus, twenty-three, was dead.

1938   Composes a prison play, *The Great Disobedience*, and revises *They Too Arise* as *The Grass Still Grows*. Graduates from the University of Michigan with a BA in English. Joins the Federal Theater Project in New York to write radio plays and scripts.

1939   The Federal Theater Project is shut down by conservative forces in Congress, and Miller goes on relief. Writes *Listen My Children* and *You're Next* with his friend and fellow

Michigan alumnus, Norman Rosten. *William Ireland's Confession* is broadcast on the Columbia Workshop.

1940   Marries Mary Grace Slattery, his college sweetheart at the University of Michigan. They move into a small apartment at 62 Montague Street in Brooklyn Heights. Writes *The Golden Years*, a play about Montezuma, Cortez, and the European conquest and corruption of Mexico. *The Pussycat and the Plumber Who Was a Man* airs on CBS Radio. Makes a trip to North Carolina to collect dialect speech for the Folk Division of the Library of Congress.

1941–   Works as a shipfitter's helper on the night shift at the
43   Brooklyn Navy Yard repairing battle-scarred war vessels from the North Atlantic fleet. Finishes additional radio plays, including *The Eagle's Nest* and *The Four Freedoms*. Completes *The Half-Bridge*. The one-act *That They May Win* is produced in New York.

1944   Daughter Jane is born. Prepares Ferenc Molnar's *The Guardsman* and Jane Austen's *Pride and Prejudice* for radio adaptation, and continues his own writing for the medium. Tours army camps in preparation for the draft of a screenplay called *The Story of G.I. Joe*, based on news reports written by the popular war correspondent Ernie Pyle (withdraws from the project when his role as author is compromised). Publishes *Situation Normal ...*, a book about this experience that highlights the real challenges returning soldiers encountered on re-entering civilian life. Dedicates the book to his brother, 'Lieutenant Kermit Miller, United States Infantry', a war hero. *The Man Who Had All the Luck* opens on Broadway but closes after six performances, including two previews. The play receives the Theater Guild National Award.

1945   Publishes *Focus*, a novel about anti-Semitism and moral blindness set in and around New York. His article 'Should Ezra Pound Be Shot?' appears in *New Masses*.

1946   Adapts *Three Men on a Horse* by George Abbott and John C. Holm for radio.
1947 *All My Sons* opens in New York and receives the New York Drama Critics' Circle Award; the Donaldson Award and the first Tony Award for best author. His son Robert is born. Moves with his family to a converted carriage house he purchases at 31 Grace Court in Brooklyn

Heights. Also buys a new car, a Studebaker, and a farmhouse in Roxbury, Connecticut. Writes the article 'Subsidized Theater' for the *New York Times*.

1948 Builds by himself a small studio on his Connecticut property where he writes *Death of a Salesman*. Edward G. Robinson and Burt Lancaster star in the film version of *All My Sons*.

1949 *Death of a Salesman*, starring Lee J. Cobb, Arthur Kennedy, Cameron Mitchell and Mildred Dunnock opens at the Morosco Theatre in New York on 10 February. Directed by Elia Kazan with designs by Jo Mielziner, it wins the New York Drama Critics' Circle Award, the Donaldson Prize, the Antoinette Perry Award, the Theatre Club Award and the Pulitzer Prize. His essay 'Tragedy and the Common Man' is printed in the *New York Times*. Attends the pro-Soviet Cultural and Scientific Conference for World Peace at the Waldorf-Astoria Hotel to chair a panel with Clifford Odets and Dimitri Shostakovich.

1950 Adaptation of Henrik Ibsen's *An Enemy of the People* produced on Broadway starring Fredric March and Florence Henderson ('I have made no secret of my early love for Ibsen's work'). First sound recording of *Death of a Salesman*. *The Hook*, a film script about graft and corruption in the closed world of longshoremen in the Red Hook section of Brooklyn, fails to reach production after backers yield to pressure from the House Committee on Un-American Activities. *On the Waterfront*, the Budd Schulberg–Elia Kazan collaboration featuring Marlon Brando, changes the setting to Hoboken, New Jersey, but is developed from the same concept, and is released four years later.

1951 Meets Marilyn Monroe. Fredric March in the role of Willy Loman for Columbia Pictures in the first film version of *Death of a Salesman*. Joseph Buloff translates the play into Yiddish; his production runs in New York and introduces Miller's play to Buenos Aires.

1952 Drives to Salem, Massachusetts, and visits the Historical Society, where he reads documents and researches the material he will use in *The Crucible*. Breaks with Kazan over the director's cooperation with HUAC.

1953 *The Crucible* wins the Donaldson Award and the Antoinette Perry Award when it opens in New York at the Martin Beck Theatre. Directs *All My Sons* in Arden, Delaware.

1954   US State Department denies Miller a passport to attend
the Belgian premiere of *The Crucible* in Brussels ('I wasn't
embarrassed for myself; I was embarrassed for my
country'). NBC broadcasts the first radio production of
Death of a Salesman. Mingei Theater stages first Japanese
translation of *Salesman* in Tokyo, where the play is
received as a cautionary tale about the 'salaryman'.

1955   The one-act version of *A View from the Bridge* opens in New
York on a double-bill with *A Memory of Two Mondays*.
HUAC pressurises city officials to withdraw permission
for Miller to make a film about juvenile delinquency set in
New York.

1956   Lives in Nevada for six weeks in order to divorce Mary
Slattery. Marries Marilyn Monroe. Subpoenaed to appear
before HUAC on 21 June, he refuses to name names.
Accepts an honorary degree as Doctor of Human Letters
from his alma mater, the University of Michigan. Jean-Paul
Sartre writes screenplay for French adaptation of *The
Crucible*, called *Les Sorcieres de Salem*; the film stars Yves
Montand and Simone Signoret. Travels with Monroe to
England, where he meets Laurence Olivier, her co-star in
The Prince and the Showgirl. Peter Brook directs revised two-
act version of *A View from the Bridge* in London at the New
Watergate Theatre Club, as censors determined it could
not be performed in public. 'Once Eddie had been
squarely placed in his social context, among his people,'
Miller noted, 'the myth-like feeling of the story emerged of
itself … Red Hook is full of Greek tragedies.'

1957   Cited for contempt of Congress for refusing to co-operate
with HUAC. On the steps of the United States Congress,
and with Monroe on his arm, he vows to appeal against
the conviction. Monroe buys all members of Congress a
year's subscription to *I.F. Stone's Weekly*. First television
production of *Death of a Salesman* (ITA, UK). *Arthur Miller's
Collected Plays* is published, and his short story, 'The
Misfits', appears in *Esquire Magazine*.

1958–   The US Court of Appeals overturns his conviction
59   for contempt of Congress. Elected to the National
Institute of Arts and Letters and receives the Gold Medal
for Drama.

1961   Miller and Monroe divorce (granted in Mexico on the
grounds of 'incompatibility'). *The Misfits*, a black-and-

white film directed by John Huston featuring the actress
in her first serious dramatic role, is released for wide
distribution. Miller calls his scenario 'an eastern western'
and bases the plot on his short story of the same name.
Co-stars include Clark Gable, Montgomery Clift, Eli
Wallach and Thelma Ritter. *The Crucible: An Opera in Four
Acts* by Robert Ward and Bernard Stambler is recorded.
Sidney Lumet directs a movie version of *A View from the
Bridge* with Raf Vallone and Carol Lawrence. Miller's
mother, Augusta, dies.

1962   Marries Austrian-born Inge Morath, a photographer with
Magnum, the agency founded in 1947 by Henri Cartier-
Bresson. Marilyn Monroe, aged thirty-six, dies. His
daughter, Rebecca Augusta, is born in September. NBC
broadcasts an adaptation of *Focus* with James Whitmore
and Colleen Dewhurst.

1963   Publishes a children's book, *Jane's Blanket*. Returns to Ann
Arbor to deliver annual Hopwood Awards lecture, 'On
Recognition'.

1964   Visits the Mauthausen death camp with Inge Morath and
covers the Nazi trials in Frankfurt, Germany, for the *New
York Herald Tribune*. Reconciles with Kazan. *Incident at Vichy*,
whose through-line is 'It's not your guilt I want, it's your
responsibility', opens in New York, as does *After the Fall*. The
former is the first of the playwright's works to be banned in
the Soviet Union. The latter Miller says 'is not about
Marilyn' and that she is 'hardly the play's *raison d'etre*'.

1965   Elected president of PEN, the international organisation
of writers dedicated to fighting all forms of censorship.
American premiere of the two-act version of *A View from
the Bridge* is performed Off-Broadway. Laurence Olivier's
production of *The Crucible*, starring Colin Blakely and
Joyce Redman, is staged in London at the Old Vic by the
National Theatre. Returns to Ann Arbor, where his
daughter Jane is now a student, to participate in the first
teach-in in the US concerning the Vietnam conflict.

1966   First sound recording of *A View from the Bridge*. In Rome
Marcello Mastroianni and Monica Vitti play the parts of
Quentin and Maggie in Franco Zeffirelli's Italian
production of *After the Fall*. Miller's father, Isidore, dies.

1967   *I Don't Need You Any More*, a collection of short stories, is
published. Sound recording of *Incident at Vichy*. Television

production of *The Crucible* is broadcast on CBS. Visits
Moscow and tries to persuade Soviet writers to join PEN.
Playwright-in-Residence at the University of Michigan.
His son, Daniel, is born in January.

1968   *The Price*, which the playwright called 'a quartet', 'the most
specific play I've ever written', opens on Broadway. Sound
recording of *After the Fall*. Attends the Democratic National
Convention in Chicago as a delegate from Roxbury,
Connecticut. Leads peace march against the war in South-
East Asia with the Reverend Sloan Coffin, Jr, at Yale
University in New Haven. *Death of a Salesman* sells its
millionth copy.

1969   *In Russia*, a collaborative project with text by Miller and
photography by Morath, is published. Visits Prague in a
show of support for Czech writers; meets Vaclav Havel.
Retires as president of PEN.

1970   Miller's works are banned in the Soviet Union, a result of
his efforts to free dissident writers. *Fame* and *The Reason
Why*, two one-act plays, are produced; the latter is filmed
at his home in Connecticut.

1971   Television productions of *A Memory of Two Mondays* on
PBS and *The Price* on NBC. Sound recording of *An Enemy
of the People*. *The Portable Arthur Miller* is published.

1972   *The Creation of the World and Other Business* opens at the
Schubert Theatre in New York on 30 November. Attends
the Democratic National Convention in Miami as a
delegate. First sound recording of *The Crucible*.

1973   PBS broadcasts Stacy Keach's television adaptation of
Incident at Vichy, with Harris Yulin as Leduc. Champions
the case of Peter Reilly, an eighteen-year-old falsely
convicted of manslaughter for his mother's murder; four
years later, all charges are dismissed. *After the Fall* with
Faye Dunaway is televised on NBC. Teaches mini-course
at the University of Michigan; students perform early
drafts of scenes from *The American Clock*.

1974   *Up from Paradise*, musical version of *The Creation of the World
and Other Business*, is staged at the Power Center for the
Performing Arts at the University of Michigan. With
music by Stanley Silverman and cover design by Al
Hirschfield, Miller calls it his 'heavenly cabaret'.

1977   A second collaborative project with Inge Morath, *In the
Country*, is published. Petitions the Czech government to

halt arrests of dissident writers. The *Archbishop's Ceiling* opens at the Kennedy Center in Washington, DC. Miller said he wanted to dramatise 'what happens ... when people know they are ... at all times talking to Power, whether through a bug or a friend who really is an informer'.

1978   *The Theater Essays of Arthur Miller* is published. NBC broadcasts the film of *Fame* starring Richard Benjamin. Belgian National Theatre mounts the twenty-fifth anniversary production of *The Crucible*; this time Miller can attend.

1979   *Chinese Encounters*, with Inge Morath, is published. Michael Rudman directs a major revival of *Death of a Salesman* at the National Theatre in London, with Warren Mitchell as Willy Loman.

1980   *Playing for Time*, the film based on Fania Fenelon's autobiography *The Musicians of Auschwitz*, is broadcast nationally on CBS, with Vanessa Redgrave and Jane Alexander. ('I tried to treat it as a story meaningful to the survivors, by which I mean all of us. I didn't want it to be a mere horror story.') *The American Clock* has its first performance at the Spoleto Festival in South Carolina, then opens in New York with the playwright's sister, Joan Copeland, as Rose Baum, a role based on their mother. Miller sees his play as 'a mural', 'a mosaic', 'a story of America talking to itself ... There's never been a society that hasn't had a clock running on it, and you can't help wondering – How long?'

1981   Second volume of *Arthur Miller's Collected Plays* is published. Delivers keynote address on the fiftieth anniversary of the Hopwood Awards Program in Ann Arbor.

1982   Two one-act plays that represent 'the colors of memory', *Elegy for a Lady* and *Some Kind of Love Story*, are produced as a double-bill at the Long Wharf Theatre in Connecticut under the title *2 by A.M.*

1983   Directs *Death of a Salesman* at the People's Art Theatre in Beijing, part of a cultural exchange to mark the early stage of the opening of diplomatic relations between the United States and the People's Republic of China. Ying Ruocheng plays Willy Loman in his own Chinese translation. *I Think About You a Great Deal*, a monologue written as a tributre to Vaclav Havel, appears in *Cross Currents*, University of Michigan.

1984   *'Salesman' in Beijing* is published. The texts of *Elegy for a Lady* and *Some Kind of Love Story* are printed under a new title, *Two-Way Mirror*. Receives Kennedy Center Honors for lifetime achievement. Reworks the script of *The American Clock* for Peter Wood's London production at the National Theatre.

1985   Twenty-five million viewers see Dustin Hoffman play Willy Loman, with John Malkovich as Biff and Kate Reid as Linda in the production of *Death of a Salesman* shown on CBS. Goes to Turkey with Harold Pinter for PEN as an ambassador for freedom of speech. Serves as delegate at a meeting of Soviet and American writers in Vilnius, Lithuania, where he attacks Russian authorities for their continuing anti-Semitism and persecution of *samizdat* writers. *The Archbishop's Ceiling* is produced in the UK by the Bristol Old Vic. Completes adaptation of *Playing for Time* as a stage play.

1986   One of fifteen writers and scientists invited to meet Mikhail Gorbachev to discuss Soviet policies. The Royal Shakespeare Company uses a revised script of *The Archbishop's Ceiling* for its London production in the Barbican Pit.

1987   Miller publishes *Timebends: A Life*, his autobiography. Characterising it as 'a preemptive strike' against future chroniclers, he discusses his relationship with Marilyn Monroe in public for the first time. *Clara* and *I Can't Remember Anything* open as a double-bill at Lincoln Center in New York under the title *Danger: Memory!* Broadcasts of *The Golden Years* on BBC Radio and Jack O'Brien's television production of *All My Sons* on PBS. Michael Gambon stars as Eddie Carbone in Alan Ayckbourn's intimate production of *A View from the Bridge* at the National Theatre in London. University of East Anglia names its site for American Studies the Arthur Miller Centre.

1988   Publishes 'Waiting for the Teacher', a nineteen-stanza free-verse poem, in *Ha'aretz*, the Tel Aviv-based liberal newspaper, on the occasion of the fiftieth anniversary of the founding of the State of Israel.

1990   *Everybody Wins*, directed by Karel Reisz with Debra

Winger and Nick Nolte, is released: 'Through the evolution of the story – a murder that took place before the story opens – we will be put through an exercise in experiencing reality and unreality.' Television production of *An Enemy of the People* on PBS. Josette Simon plays Maggie as a sultry jazz singer in Michael Blakemore's London revival of *After the Fall* at the National Theatre, where *The Crucible* also joins the season's repertory in Howard Davies's production starring Zoë Wannamaker and Tom Wilkinson. Updated version of *The Man Who Had All the Luck* is staged by Paul Unwin in a joint production by the Bristol Old Vic and the Young Vic in London.

1991   *The Last Yankee* premieres as a one-act play. *The Ride Down Mount Morgan*, 'a moral farce', has its world premiere in London: 'The play is really a kind of nightmare.' Television adaptation of *Clara* on the Arts & Entertainment Network. Receives Mellon Bank Award for lifetime achievement in the humanities.

1992   *Homely Girl, A Life* is published with artwork by Louise Bourgeois in a Peter Blum edition. Writes satirical op-ed piece for the *New York Times* urging an end to capital punishment in the US.

1993   Expanded version of *The Last Yankee* opens at the Manhattan Theatre Club in New York. Television version of *The American Clock* on TNT with the playwright's daughter, Rebecca, in the role of Edie.

1994   *Broken Glass*, a work 'full of ambiguities' that takes 'us back to the time when the social contract was being torn up', has a pre-Broadway run at the Long Wharf Theatre in Connecticut; opens at the Booth Theatre in New York on 24 April. David Thacker's London production wins the Olivier Award for Best Play.

1995   Tributes to the playwright on the occasion of his eightieth birthday are held in England and the US. Receives William Inge Festival Award for Distinguished Achievement in American Theater. *Homely Girl, A Life and Other Stories*, is published. In England the collection appears under the title *Plain Girl*. Darryl V. Jones directs a production of *A View from the Bridge* in Washington, DC, and resets the play in a community of Domincan immigrants. The Arthur Miller Society is founded by Steve Centola.

1996   Revised and expanded edition of *The Theater Essays of Arthur Miller* is published. Receives the Edward Albee Last Frontier Playwright Award. Rebecca Miller and Daniel Day-Lewis are married.

1997   *The Crucible*, produced by the playwright's son, Robert A. Miller, is released for wide distribution and is nominated for an Academy Award. Revised version of *The Ride Down Mount Morgan* performed at the Williamstown Playhouse in Massachusetts. BBC airs television version of *Broken Glass*, with Margot Leicester and Henry Goodman repeating their roles from the award-winning London production.

1998   *Mr Peters' Connections* opens in New York with Peter Falk. Revival of *A View from the Bridge* by the Roundabout Theatre Company wins two Tony Awards. Revised version of *The Ride Down Mount Morgan* on Broadway. Miller is named Distinguished Inaugural Senior Fellow of the American Academy in Berlin.

1999   Robert Falls's fiftieth anniversary production of *Death of a Salesman*, featuring Brian Dennehy as Willy Loman, moves from the Goodman Theater in Chicago and opens on Broadway, where it wins the Tony Award for Best Revival of a Play. Co-authors the libretto with Arnold Weinstein for William Bolcom's opera of *A View from the Bridge*, which has its world premiere at the Lyric Opera of Chicago.

2000   Patrick Stewart reprises his role as Lyman Felt in *The Ride Down Mount Morgan* on Broadway, where *The Price* is also revived (with Harris Yulin). Major eighty-fifth birthday celebrations are organised by Christopher Bigsby at the University of East Anglia and by Enoch Brater at the University of Michigan, where plans are announced to build a new theatre named in his honour; it opens officially on 29 March 2007 ('whoever thought when I was saving $500 to come to the University of Michigan that it would come to this'). 'Up to a certain point the human being is completely unpredictable. That's what keeps me going … You live long enough, you don't rust.' *Echoes Down the Corridor*, a collection of essays from 1944 to 2000, is published. Miller and Morath travel to Cuba with William and Rose Styron and meet Fidel Castro and the Colombian writer Gabriel García Márquez.

2001   Williamstown Theater Festival revives *The Man Who Had All the Luck*. Laura Dern and William H. Macy star in a film based on the 1945 novel *Focus*. Miller is named the Jefferson Lecturer in the Humanities by NEH and receives the John H. Finley Award for Exemplary Service to New York City. His speech *On Politics and the Art of Acting* is published.

2002   Revivals in New York of *The Man Who Had All the Luck* and *The Crucible*, the latter with Liam Neeson as John Proctor. *Resurrection Blues* has its world premiere at the Guthrie Theatre in Minneapolis. Miller receives a major international award in Spain, the Premio Principe de Asturias de las Letras. Death of Inge Morath.

2003   Awarded the Jerusalem Prize. His brother, Kermit Miller, dies on 17 October. *The Price* is performed at the Tricycle Theatre in London.

2004   *Finishing the Picture* opens at the Goodman Theatre in Chicago. *After the Fall* revived in New York. Appears on a panel at the University of Michigan with Mark Lamos, who directs students in scenes from Miller's rarely performed plays.

2005   Miller dies of heart failure in his Connecticut home on 10 February. Public memorial service is held on 9 May at the Majestic Theatre in New York, with 1,500 in attendance. Asked what he wanted to be remembered for, the playwright said, 'A few good parts for actors.'

Plot

Act One

The curtain rises on a summer Sunday morning in a suburban 'back yard', the garden at the back of the house. It is worth noting that this is the outskirts of a town, not a big city; these are small-town people in America's heartland – culturally, as well as geographically.

Joe Keller, the play's pivotal character, is sitting in a lawn chair reading the newspaper. His next-door neighbour, Jim Bayliss, a doctor, is staring at a tree that blew over in last night's storm. They are joined by another neighbour, Frank Lubey. Joe comments on the want ads, revealing both his interest in what people buy and his ignorance of the world, a lack of sophistication he is conscious of, although not embarrassed by. The conversation quickly turns to the fallen tree, a memorial for Larry, Joe's eldest son who was reported missing in action three years before during the Second World War. Frank remarks on the coincidence of the timing – the tree having fallen in the same month as Larry's birthday – revealing that, at Kate's request, he is creating a horoscope for Larry, part of Kate's attempt to 'prove' that Larry might still return home alive.

Joe reveals that Ann, Larry's former fiancée, arrived the night before for a visit. She and her family used to live in the house now occupied by the Bayliss family. Jim's wife Sue, a former nurse, interrupts their conversation by calling her husband to the phone, and their continuing squabble about Jim's professional life reveals her worries about money – she wants him to see any patient who will pay (this was still the era of doctors who made house calls) and Jim reveals his impatience with hypochondriacs. Next, Lydia, Frank's wife, arrives, complaining about a broken toaster; she wonders aloud if Ann has recovered from Larry's death, marvelling that in the few years that have passed since then, she herself has had three babies; Joe remarks that 'it [war] changed all the tallies', that he had two sons and now has one.

Enter Chris, the son he still has, with his morning coffee; he chooses the book-review section of the newspaper which establishes his interest in intellectual matters. Bert, a neighbourhood child, arrives, continuing the make-believe game Joe invented for the local boys: they are his 'policemen', inspecting the neighbourhood for signs of wrongdoing. This game, we will learn, is a result of Joe's return to the neighbourhood after the factory scandal: his partner, Steve, Ann's father, went to prison while Joe was exonerated. The game evolved from the neighbourhood boys' fascination with this brush with the law. Chris tells Joe that Kate was outside in the yard the previous night and saw the tree crack and fall. They discuss her need to believe that Larry is still alive and Chris explains that they should have made her confront the reality of his death that they have both accepted. Chris then tells his father that he plans to ask Ann to marry him, knowing that his parents feel she is still 'Larry's girl'. This leads to Chris's declaration that if his parents can't accept his marriage to Ann, he will leave them and the business and move away. Joe is thunderstruck by this, protesting that his years of work in the business have all been for Chris.

Kate comes out of the house, oddly preoccupied, complaining of a headache. Surprisingly, she is pleased that the tree blew down, reasoning that planting it as a memorial for Larry was premature, that this is a sign that Larry is still alive. She recounts her dream the night before in which Larry called to her from a low-flying plane. Kate insists that the timing of Ann's visit and the fact that Ann has remained unmarried support her belief, and she is clearly suspicious of Chris's interest in his brother's fiancée. As a way to change the subject and the mood, Chris suggests they all go out for dinner and dancing that night, although once Chris goes into the house, Kate's smile vanishes and she continues, with great urgency and distress, to tell her husband of her uneasiness about Ann's arrival. They seem to touch on what will become the central fact of the play – although we cannot know this yet – when she says 'You above all have got to believe . . .' and Joe replies, 'What does that mean, me above all?' Bert rushes into the yard and distracts them (and us) from this crucial conversation. Kate is distraught about the game Joe and Bert play, 'that whole jail business', and Joe asks, significantly, but apparently indignantly, 'What have I got to hide?'

Finally, Ann appears, looking lovely, with news of her family: this is where we get the first clue that her father, Joe's former business partner, is in prison. Ann tells Kate that she does not believe Larry is alive and is no longer waiting for him. Kate argues that she has to keep believing he is alive: 'That's why there's God.' Frank returns, borrows a ladder, sympathises with Ann about her father. Ann recalls the past, when the neighbours called Joe and her father Steve 'Murderers!', but Joe assures her that it is all forgotten, and that all those accusatory neighbours now play poker on Saturday nights in the Kellers' back yard.

Joe traces the events of the past when he walked down the street after he was released from prison, facing down his neighbours on their verandas, all of whom believed he was guilty despite the court's exoneration. 'Fourteen months later I had one of the best shops in the state again, a respected man again; bigger than ever.' Ann is amazed that Joe doesn't hold a grudge against her father who was found guilty of shipping damaged airplane parts to the US Army. Ann discloses that neither she nor her brother has seen or written to their father since the trial.

Joe then explains his version of how the signal event of the past happened: the cracks in the cylinder heads were discovered, the pressure from the Army to deliver the goods, Steve's decision to cover up the flaws and ship them out. Joe asserts that he was at home sick that day, and that it was simply a 'mistake' on Steve's part.

Ann and Chris confess their love for each other. Chris tells her about his painful experiences in the war. Many of his men were killed, though they displayed their loyalty to each other, a willingness to sacrifice themselves rather than be selfish, revealing to Chris the 'one new thing' made out

of all the war's destruction: 'responsibility. Man for man.'
He explains his disillusionment when he returned home to
work in his father's factory, feeling 'ashamed' because the
rat-race was still on. America seemed to have learned
nothing from the war except how profitable it was.

Joe returns to the yard to find Chris and Ann in an
embrace, and Chris tells him they are getting married. They
decide to tell Kate later. He announces that Ann's brother,
George, has telephoned. While she is in the house talking to
George on the phone, Joe urges Chris to enjoy their
factory's financial success, and tells him he wants to change
the business's name to his son's. Chris deflects the offer. Ann
returns to the yard to announce that George, who is now a
lawyer, is arriving by train that evening, having just visited
their father in prison. Kate, who has now come out of the
house, is very frightened and warns Joe to 'be smart'.

Act Two

It is early evening of the same day, and Chris has been
sawing apart the broken tree. Kate and Joe are both worried
about George's imminent visit, suspicious that he – and
perhaps Ann, too – hates the Kellers because Steve took all
the blame and punishment. Sue and Ann discuss the
prospect of Chris and Ann's marriage, and Sue reveals her
bitterness about her own marriage. She hopes Ann and
Chris will live elsewhere since Chris's nobility, what Sue
calls his 'phony idealism', makes Jim feel trapped and
dissatisfied. Sue further reveals that everyone knows 'Joe
pulled a fast one to get out of jail', and casts doubt on Ann's
certainty that Chris wouldn't work for a firm built on blood
money.

When Joe appears after his nap, Chris and Ann gently
mock his lack of education; he then cleverly suggests setting
up George in legal practice locally, and proffers the
possibility of Steve's return to the firm when he finishes his
prison term, causing Chris to explode angrily.

Lydia arrives to fix Kate's hair for the planned night out.
Jim arrives, having left George in the car, and warns Chris

that George has 'blood in his eye'. George, who has just
visited Steve in prison, tells Chris and Ann the truth of the
events of that fateful day: Joe told him to ship the damaged
cylinder heads. Chris becomes enraged, denying George's
accusations.

But once Kate enters, George is disarmed by her affection
and by nostalgia for the innocent pre-war past when they
were all children. Joe, too, manipulates George, using
George's contempt for his father to turn the argument
around. But then Joe casually brags that he has never been
sick – and suddenly they all freeze with the revelation that
gives the lie to Joe's claim he was too ill to go into work the
day Steve shipped the damaged goods.

Frank bursts into the scene, excited to announce that
Larry's horoscope 'proves' that he should still be alive.
George leaves; Kate tells Ann to leave, saying she is still
'Larry's girl'. In the ensuing argument, Kate tells Chris that
unless he believes Larry is still alive, he condemns his father
as his murderer. Chris confronts Joe with the truth. Joe
admits wrongdoing, but insists it was all so that Chris would
inherit a successful business. Chris is horrified.

Act Three
In the middle of the night, Kate is sitting outside waiting for
Chris who has disappeared; Jim joins her and reveals that
he has always known of Joe's guilt. Joe enters, desperate for
advice about what to do. She suggests that Chris might be
mollified by Joe's willingness to admit guilt and take his
punishment by saying he will go to prison. Kate explains
that to Chris there is 'something bigger than the family', and
Joe replies, in a remark that foreshadows the end of the
play, 'if there's something bigger than that I'll put a bullet in
my head!'

Ann enters, and offers Kate a deal: she will not prosecute
Joe in exchange for Kate's admission that Larry is dead and
that Chris is free to marry her. When Kate refuses, Ann
shows her Larry's last letter explaining that he had just read
the news of the twenty-one pilots killed as a result of his

father's faulty airplane parts, and announcing his suicide. Chris returns, saying that he is going away and Ann shows the letter to him. He reads it to Joe. Joe learns the play's lesson of moral responsibility for the family of man, not just one's own family. Chris demands more than 'sorry' from his father who goes into the house, presumably to get ready to leave for prison, and shoots himself.

Chris is desperate with grief and Kate tries to absolve him with her final injunction, 'Forget now. Live.'

Commentary

Context

Social history

A play about war-profiteering opening in 1947, when the Second World War had so recently ended, must have been pointedly painful to the audience, considering how many had experienced similar losses of a son, a brother, a fiancé. Of course, even for those whose circumstances did not resemble *All My Sons'*, the play's lesson is that they are 'all our sons' and thus that the grief and culpability are communal. The play's shocking revelations and Miller's insistence that we must take responsibility for our actions provide a lesson about the destructive self-interest and the greed that drives capitalism, sacrificing human values to material values. This moral force resonates in whatever the current social context is, although it must have been additionally vivid for people who had recently endured the Great Depression as well as the Second World War. In his Introduction to *Plays: One* (1988), Miller writes that *All My Sons* was 'conceived in wartime and begun in wartime . . . at a time when all public voices were announcing the arrival of that great day when industry and labor were one, my personal experience was daily demonstrating that beneath the slogans very little had changed' (22).

In gauging the temper of the times further, it is interesting to note that in 1942, President Franklin Delano Roosevelt ratcheted up industrial mobilisation for the war, requiring, among other equipment, 60,000 new aircraft. In one of his famous 'Fireside Chats' radio broadcasts in 1942, he said, 'In the last war, I had seen great factories; but until I saw some of the new present-day plants, I had not thoroughly visualised our American war effort . . . The United States has been at war for only ten months, and is engaged in the

enormous task of multiplying its armed forces many times.
We are by no means at full production level yet.' By 1943
the government raised the production goals to 125,000 new
aircraft. This is the source of the pressure Joe Keller felt;
George explains his father's version of what happened once
the defects were discovered and he telephoned Joe to come
to the plant: 'No sign of Joe. So Dad called again. By this
time he had over a hundred defectives. The Army was
screaming for stuff and Dad didn't have anything to ship. So
Joe told him [. . .] to cover up the cracks in any way he
could, and ship them out.' Joe explains this same
desperation near the end of the play: 'I'm in business, a man
is in business; a hundred and twenty cracked, you're out of
business; [. . .] your stuff is no good; they close you up, they
tear up your contracts, what the hell's it to them?'

In Miller's 1944 *Situation Normal . . .*, which he called 'a
book of reportage', he wrote, 'A man who has known the
thrill of giving himself does not soon forget it. It leaves him
with a thirst. A thirst for a wider life, a more exciting life, a
life that demands all he can give. Civilian life in America is
private, it is always striving for exclusiveness. Our lifelong
boast is that we got ahead of the next guy, excluded him.
We have always believed in the fiction – and often damned
our own belief – that if every man privately takes care of his
own interests, the community and the nation will prosper
and be safe.' In *Timebends* (1987), his autobiography, Miller's
comment on this is significant: 'Though unable to define it
in words, they [soldiers] shared a conviction that somehow
decency was at stake in this grandest slaughter in history'
(277).

In 1947, after *All My Sons* opened on Broadway, Miller's
name appeared in an ad in the newspaper the *Daily Worker*
(published in New York by the Communist Party) protesting
against the treatment of Gerhard Eisler, an anti-fascist
German refugee. Miller auctioned off a manuscript of *All
My Sons* to support Progressive Citizens of America. During
this same year, the Civil Affairs Division of the American
Military refused to allow the production of *All My Sons* in
occupied Europe, citing its negative criticism of American

society. In *Echoes Down the Corridor* (2000), Miller noted that
'I wrote *All My Sons* during the war, expecting much trouble,
but the war ended just as I was completing the play, leaving
some room for the unsayable, which everyone knew – that
the war had made some people illicit, sometimes criminal
fortunes' (xi). Similar to this is Miller's recollection of
seeing the play in Jerusalem in 1977: 'the audience sat
watching it with an intensifying terror that was quite
palpable. On our right sat the president of Israel, Ephraim
Katzir, on the left the prime minister, Yitzhak Rabin',
who explained what Miller felt to be 'an almost religious
quality' in the audience's attention: 'Because this is a
problem in Israel – boys are out there day and night dying
in planes and on the ground, and back here people are
making a lot of money. So it might as well be an Israeli play'
(*Timebends*, 135).

There are two accounts of the source of the play's plot:
one is that Miller read about the Wright Aeronautics
Corporation of Ohio (the state where the play takes place);
the company affixed 'Passed' tags on defective airplane
engines, having bribed Army inspectors; the other source is
a story Miller heard in his living room, when 'a pious lady
from the Middle West told of a family in her neighbourhood
which had been destroyed when the daughter turned the
father in to the authorities on discovering that he had been
selling faulty machinery to the Army. The war was then in
full blast. By the time she had finished the tale I had
transformed the daughter into a son and the climax of the
second act was full and clear in my mind' (*Plays: One*, 17). It
is worth noting Miller's shift from daughter to son: perhaps
nothing marks twentieth-century American drama more
than the highly charged and very male family battles
between sons and fathers, brothers and brothers; note that,
like O'Neill's *A Long Day's Journey into Night*, Williams's *Cat on
a Hot Tin Roof*, Shepard's *True West*, Parks's *Topdog/Underdog*
– an obviously abbreviated list which nevertheless stretches
through the entire century – the controversy is almost
always between men and always about money. Like all these
plays, *All My Sons* is also about two brothers and their father

and money, as are two of Miller's own subsequent plays, *Death of a Salesman* and *The Price*.

In *Timebends*, Miller remembers asking his cousin, 'What did your pop want?' His answer: 'He wanted a business for us. So we could all work together [. . .] a business for the boys' (130). Miller realised that his uncle Manny, a 'homely, ridiculous little man had after all never ceased to struggle for a certain victory, the only kind open to him in this society – selling to achieve his lost self as a man with his name and his sons' names on a business of his own'.

In the course of Act One's opening desultory conversation, all three men reveal a reflexive and cheap cynicism about the news: weather reports are automatically discounted as inaccurate, news is automatically assumed to be bad. Note that this is in the ease of post-war America; we can assume that only a few years earlier, during the war, the news was bad in an entirely different way, specifically when it reported the scandal of Joe's factory having shipped the faulty airplane parts that led to the planes crashing and deaths of twenty-one pilots – the newspaper account which caused Larry's suicide. Note that later in Act One, when Chris tells his father that their dishonesty in not discouraging his mother's false hope that Larry is still alive and will return home has been a mistake, Joe's reply is 'The trouble is the goddam newspapers', referring to reports of other missing soldiers who have come home.

The contemporary world has no shortage of bad news. Public endangerment scandals re-inform the play with each re-reading or revival, from the destruction of the spaceship *Challenger* due to faulty O rings, to the twenty-year Canadian Red Cross blood-distribution disgrace which infected people with HIV, to the 2008 outrage in China over milk tainted with melamine causing 300,000 infants to sicken, to the 2009 US epidemic of salmonella caused by peanut butter shipped despite contamination warnings. And, most spectacularly, the global economic crisis begun in 2008 and Bernard Madoff's role in it[1]; his scam wrecked hundreds of

---

[1] The trusted Wall Street broker whose $50 billion Ponzi scheme cheated investors around the world.

thousands of lives, institutions, and corporations, and it is worth noting for our purposes of comparison to *All My Sons* that Madoff's two sons, who ran the company's market-making and proprietary units, said that their father kept them in the dark about the secret business, a 'dark' which may resemble Chris's willed ignorance. Money, as Miller's play warns us, is always likely to triumph over decency until the world learns that they are 'all our sons'. As Miller wrote in *Timebends*, 'I could not imagine a theatre worth my time that did not want to change the world.'

Theatrical history
In the stream of the history of great American dramatists, Miller follows Eugene O'Neill. But where O'Neill's tragic vision suggests that people are doomed – by temperament, by events they cannot control, and by the weight of the past – Miller's is a fighting play, insisting that we can live more moral lives if only we acknowledge our place in the family of man. The tragic lesson is always that that understanding comes too late. Whether this means that *All My Sons* is to be read as a tragedy largely depends on the reader's (and, in production, the director's) optimism: *can* we 'be better'? In the wider, longer stream of the history of great Western dramatists, Miller follows Ibsen, whose plays show that the societal context inevitably influences individual lives and that social context can be altered by social action; thus, although the issues of women's rights and, indeed, all human rights have not been solved in the nearly 150 years since *A Doll's House*, significant changes in both ethics and legislation have achieved some social progress.

In theatrical production, *All My Sons* requires a tricky combination of ensemble work – the cast must seem to be a family, a neighbourhood, creating the comfort of people who are familiar with each other on a daily basis, while also creating a sense of alienation, the very opposite of ensemble. *All My Sons* is about what Miller called 'unrelatedness', the mistake of believing that responsibility stops at the edge of your back yard. And, unlike O'Neill, Miller writes realistic, grounded language, creating speakable dialogue that allows the audience to identify further with the characters in a crucial emotional as well as thematic arc. They sound familiar. They sound like an old-fashioned version of us.

In *Timebends*, Miller recalls his disappointment when Herman Shumlin, Lillian Hellman's producer and director, having read *All My Sons* said he 'didn't understand it' (268). Miller defines himself, from this early moment, as a 'social playwright', like Hellman, an identity that continues in his pursuit of a production and a director, so he was naturally thrilled when both Elia Kazan and Harold Clurman, 'creators of that thirties mixture of Stanislavsky and social protest which was the real glamour' (*Timebends*, 270) were bidding for the script. When it opened on 29 January 1947, Brooks Atkinson, the powerful *New York Times* critic, praised Miller as a 'genuine new talent' and added, 'there is something uncommonly exhilarating in the spectacle of a new writer bringing unusual gifts to the theatre under the sponsorship of a director with taste and enthusiasm'; the director was Elia Kazan.

As Miller's first successful play on Broadway, *All My Sons* launched the great career and established Miller as America's social critic, the voice of a collective conscience telling us, as Chris tells his father, 'You can be better!' *All My Sons* also established Miller's style as realistic, thereby launching a commonly held error, since the plays that follow *All My Sons* depart from realism. This becomes especially interesting in the light of subsequent productions of *All My Sons*, influencing set design, lighting, sound, etc. As Miller wrote, 'No, I am not really interested in "realism". I never was. What I'm interested in is reality . . . Realism can conceal reality, perhaps a little easier than any other form, in fact' (Roudané, 362).

Themes

Time

In *Timebends*, Miller writes about 'the hand of the distant past reach[ing] out of its grave', an image which defines the plot of *All My Sons* (as it defines the plot of Ibsen's *Ghosts*, for example), like the iron hand of the past clamped on the present and the future in O'Neill's *Long Day's Journey into Night*. In *All My Sons*, this hand of the 'distant past' substantiates Miller's theme that actions have moral consequences, and essentially builds the structure of the play on a series of surprising revelations. It is worth noting that, like O'Neill's family drama which is also about two grown sons, *All My Sons* is also, temporally, a long day's journey into night, a play which begins with the sunny optimism of morning and ends in grim darkness. Similarly, *Death of a Salesman* is a play about past events which govern the present, but in *Salesman* scenes from the past slice through the scenes in the play's present, refusing the chronological linearity of *All My Sons* and creating a visible psychological landscape.

References to time appear throughout the play: all that happened in the past – not only Joe's decision to save his business instead of lives, but also all that happened to Chris in the past in the Army. We learn about his military experience, his leadership and how his squad's self-sacrificial generosity became central to his ethics and values, and his shock and disgust at returning to a post-war world where it was business-as-usual. There is constant mention of how long Larry has been missing, how long Ann has been single, how long Chris has been waiting, how long Steve has been in prison, how long Jim's time of impassioned medical research lasted, how long the poplars have been growing, how long since Larry's memorial tree was planted.

Significantly, when George arrives, wrecked by the war, enraged by his visit to his father, brimming with accusations as well as self-recrimination, his anger and resolution are quickly defused by Kate's grape drink and her insistence that all is as it was: 'None of us changed, Georgie. We all love you.' Awash in nostalgia (the word means 'homesickness'), George caves in to her affectionate manipulation.

Imprisonment

Much of the history of modern drama could be written in scenes of entrapment; if it is the emblem of modern man's sense of impotence in the face of the enormous forces facing him, trapped as he is by history, psychology, genetics, economics, etc., then the modern stage is, necessarily, a claustrophobic arena. Beckett's *Waiting for Godot* and Sartre's *No Exit* are the paradigmatic examples. An interesting set design will allow the audience to interpret the issues central to the script: it evokes atmosphere and speaks meaning, without ever explicitly telegraphing to the audience what the play is going to be about. Although the setting often echoes the theme by trapping characters in one room (increasingly a thrifty as well as meaningful development in modern set design), in *All My Sons*, the setting is not an indoor room but a back yard. But rather than create a feeling of openness and fresh air, it fences in the family and divides neighbour from neighbour. Even as the barriers between the Kellers' yard and the Bayliss's and the Lubeys' yards are permeable – the neighbours enter and exit constantly – Miller's stage directions nevertheless specify that the 'stage is hedged on right and left by tall, closely planted poplars which lend the yard a secluded atmosphere'. Note that when Ann arrives after three years in New York, she runs to the fence and says, 'Boy, the poplars got thick, didn't they?' How symbolic this setting becomes will be reflected in the many possibilities for design choices.

The scene with Bert in Act One is a microcosm of the entire play: Bert's curiosity about the promised jail in the Keller house prompts Joe to say: 'Bert, on my word of honor, there's a jail in the basement. I showed you my gun, didn't I?' Note how much is packed into this seemingly playful line: the house is, truly, a prison; Joe's gun will be the instrument of his shame-filled and repentant suicide; and Joe's 'word of honor' is, we will learn, worthless. The scene with Bert concludes with Joe telling the boy, 'mum's the word', an unwitting comment on the family's policy of silencing the truth, and thereby denying the guilt that has festered under the surface.

Steve is, literally, in prison. Note, too, that when Sue
explains to Ann why she hopes once she and Chris marry
they will move away, Sue says, 'it's bad when a man always
sees the bars in front of him. Jim thinks he's in jail all the
time . . . My husband is unhappy with Chris around' (47).
Jim's capitulation to his imprisonment – however pragmatic,
however cynical, however sad – is revealed late in Act Two
when he reassures Kate about Chris's storming out of the
house: 'We all come back, Kate. These private little
revolutions always die. The compromise is always made. In
a peculiar way, Frank is right – every man does have a star.
The star of one's honesty. And you spend your life groping
for it, but once it's out it never lights again. I don't think he
went very far. He probably just wanted to be alone to watch
his star go out.' But Chris's star of honesty does not 'go out'
even though he may be imprisoned in other ways, especially
by his own need to be good, a need that demands that
others 'be better', as he tells his mother at the play's end.

Materialism and the American dream
The first instance of the phrase 'the American dream'
occurs in James Truslow Adams's *The Epic of America* (1933);
he defines that 'dream of a land in which life should be
better and richer and fuller for every man, with opportunity
for each according to his ability or his achievement [....]
The American dream that lured tens of millions of all
nations to our shores [. . .] has not been a dream of merely
material plenty. [. . .] It has been a dream of being able to
grow to fullest development as man and woman [. . .]
unhampered by the barriers which had slowly been erected
in older civilizations . . .'. And even in 1933 (the Great
Depression had surely challenged the American dream in
unprecedented ways), Adams laments the erosion of the
values which had constituted the societal understanding of
that dream: 'we came to insist on business and money-
making and material improvement as good in themselves
[...to] consider an unthinking optimism essential, [. . .]
regard[ing] criticism as obstructive and dangerous [. . . to]

think manners undemocratic, and a cultivated mind a
hindrance to success, a sign of inefficient effeminacy [. . . and]
size and statistics of material development came to be more
important in our eyes than quality and spiritual values . . .'.
The eerie aptness of Adams's assessment, so many decades
after it was written, suggests that the critique may be
timeless.

Destructive to society as well as to the individual,
materialism is what Miller called 'the petty business of life in
the suburbs'. In *All My Sons*, the context is the essentially
amoral post-war American prosperity (1947's economic and
physical landscape was very different in Europe to what it
was in the US). Chris's long speech to Ann tries to explain
the shock and dismay he felt when he came back from the
war: 'there was no meaning in it here; the whole thing to
them was a kind of a – bus accident . . . I felt wrong to be
alive, to open the bank-book, to drive the new car, to see the
new refrigerator' (38). The sense of corruption related to
material success is also eerily apt: Joe Keller, in Act Two,
says, 'A little man makes a mistake and they hang him by
his thumbs; the big ones become ambassadors.' Compare
this cynicism to a nearly identical remark in O'Neill's
Emperor Jones: 'For de little stealin' dey gits you in jail soon or
late. For de big stealin' dey makes you Emperor and puts
you in de Hall o' Fame when you croaks.'

Martin Esslin points out that the fundamental premises of
the Theatre of the Absurd, as set forth in his landmark book
(*The Theatre of the Absurd*, 1962; 3rd edn London: Methuen,
2001), go far towards elucidating the differences between
the American and the British societal environment. In brief,
they include: 'the sense that the certitudes and unshakable
basic assumptions of former ages have been swept away,
that they have been tested and found wanting, that they
have been discredited as cheap and somewhat childish
illusions' (23) and that such Absurdist plays 'express [. . .]
the senselessness of the human condition and the
inadequacy of the rational approach by the open
abandonment of rational devices and discursive thought. [. . .]
The Theatre of the Absurd has renounced arguing *about* the

absurdity of the human condition; it merely *presents* it in being – that is in terms of concrete stage images' (24–25).

Esslin argues that the 'dearth of examples' of Absurdist drama in the US is due to the fact that the Second World War did not happen there, since Absurdism 'springs from a feeling of deep disillusionment, the draining away of the sense of meaning and purpose in life which has been characteristic of countries like France and Britain in the years after the Second World War. In the United States there has been no corresponding loss of meaning and purpose. The American dream of the good life is still very strong' (311). Instead of despairing, Chris rails against this loss of 'meaning and purpose', refusing to relinquish belief in American progress: 'Everything was being destroyed, see, but it seemed to me that one new thing was made. A kind of . . . responsibility. Man for man.'

Joe senses this in Chris's reluctance to 'use what I made for you . . . I mean, with joy, Chris, without shame [. . .] Because sometimes I think you're . . . ashamed of the money' (41). In their horrific showdown near the play's end, Joe tells his wife, 'you wanted money, so I made money. What must I be forgiven? You wanted money, didn't you?' She replies, underlining her complicity in all this, showing that no one is pure or blameless: 'I didn't want it that way.' And Joe comes back with, 'I didn't want it that way, either! What difference is it what you want? I spoiled both of you.' Jim Bayliss's comment to Kate early in Act Three seems significant, equating materialism with madness: 'Nobody realises how many people are walking around loose, and they're cracked as coconuts. Money. Money-money-money-money. You say it long enough it doesn't mean anything. Oh, how I'd love to be around when that happens.' Kate's realistic response is, 'You're so childish, Jim!' (79).

Like *Death of a Salesman*'s Willy Loman, Joe Keller has subscribed to a set of wrong-headed and self-defeating values: the American dream has been corrupted by materialism, and those who believe in that corrupted version of the dream are, according to Miller, doomed to failure – a failure which both Joe and Willy respond to with suicide. For Willy his suicide is his last sale: his life for the insurance money to launch Biff into his 'magnificent' future; while for Joe the suicide is penance for the material greed he yielded to in the past. One could argue that Joe's death is an easy way out: an escape from repentance, guilt, apologies, years of denial of culpability, in addition to burdening his son with the guilt of having driven him to death.

Other dominant themes are discussed elsewhere in this commentary; these include:

Moral responsibility: a group of related ideas about responsibility to self and to society.

Family loyalty: this is exclusive and tribal, destructive to the universal family of man, and, as a corollary to this, the maternal is seen as primal, ruthlessly protective of the nuclear family unit.

War: Chris discovers the real nature of loyalty in the brotherhood of self-sacrificial soldiers. It is worth noting that this is not a conventional anti-war play.

Denial: the psychological self-protective device that enables self-interest. As Joe says, 'I ignore what I gotta ignore.' This theme is, obviously, fundamental to the entire play.

Fathers and sons: (Joe and Chris, Joe and Larry, Steve and George) one of the central relationships of American drama. This is a pattern particular to American drama (see p.xxvii) as well as to Miller's plays: consider the similarities to *Death of a Salesman* and *The Price*. The corollary to this theme is the theme of brothers (also dominating the aforementioned plays), often struggling – physically and/or emotionally – with each other.

Characters

Chris Keller
As one of the central and pivotal characters, Chris makes all

the plot's events happen, and thus is, perhaps, the character most representative of the playwright, whose task it is to make the play happen. On the surface, Chris is the hero: courageous in war, modest in peace, and entirely decent, a man deserving of his community's affection and admiration. But despite having been back home for several years, working in his father's factory (we never find out what it is he does there – sufficient to say that he is deeply connected to the Keller business and we presume his is a white-collar job), he seems to be merely one of the 'sons', somehow still a boy, despite his history of military bravery. The soldiers in Chris's unit, under his command, 'didn't die; they killed themselves for each other', as he tells Ann, and when one of them gave him his last pair of dry socks, he takes that as an emblem of their self-sacrificial generosity, and thus their tribute to him as their leader is, for Chris, an emblem of their goodness rather than his own. He is still troubled by their deaths, but he never indicates any inner torment about the enemy deaths he must have caused or the horrors he must have seen. He admires unselfishness, as opposed to the more aggressive, fiercer forms courage might take. His mildness extends to his love life, as we see in the scene where he kisses Ann; he is a sweet rather than a sexually passionate man. Significantly, he achieves manhood when he stands up to his mother when she tries to drive Ann away. Miller indicts the American idea of manhood as Joe defines it in his attempt to explain his past actions to Chris: 'You're a boy, what could I do! I'm in business, a man is in business' (76). Chris is not 'in business', and thus is not 'a man'. Although Joe is the designated guilty party, they are all culpable. Chris's refusal to 'see it human', as Joe pleads, is telling; his acknowledgment that Joe is 'no worse than most men but I thought you were better. I never saw you as a man. I saw you as my father (89)' shows an idealism which seems both laudable and at the same time adolescent: he is unable to view his parents as people separate from their relationship to him. That confrontation near the end continues significantly: Chris says, 'I can't look at you this way, I can't look at myself!' He then 'turns away, unable to

face Keller' (89); and that small stage direction may be
Miller's largest clue as to Chris's unacknowledged guilt.

So many grown men in Miller plays – and in American
drama generally – seem to be stuck in an arrested
adolescence: living in their parents' home, without wives or
children of their own. The Kellers' neighbour, Frank Lubey,
stands as a foil to Chris; always a year away from being
drafted into the army, he now has a wife and three children,
with a house of his own. Worth noting, too, is George's lack
of a family. As Chris tells his mother, specifically referring to
Larry's death but generally speaking of his own condition,
'We're like a railroad station waiting for a train that never
comes in' (21). The train, it turns out, will arrive in a few
minutes: enter Ann, and with her the incontrovertible
evidence of Joe's guilt and the promise of adult life for
Chris.

Chris is adored, not just by the soldiers he commanded,
but by friends and neighbours – with the significant
exception of Sue, the doctor's wife, whose self-interest,
financial as well as emotional, is undermined by Chris's
idealism: 'Chris makes people want to be better than it's
possible to be.' She feels he tempts her husband away from
the practicalities of supporting a family with the ideal of
medical research, i.e. towards self-sacrifice and away from
self-interest, towards altruism. But despite Chris's apparent
idealism, he has clearly accepted the materialistic values of
his society and the conventional male role of provider; when
Ann accepts his proposal of marriage, he is thrilled and
expresses his joy by saying, 'Oh Annie, Annie . . . I'm going
to make a fortune for you!' (38).

Chris's name is significant, since he seems to be not only
the embodiment of Christian virtues but perhaps the
embodiment of Christ. Sue tells Ann, 'I resent living next
door to the Holy Family. It makes me look like a bum, you
understand?' As Joe will plead with him near the end,
'Chris, a man can't be a Jesus in this world!' Miller has
Chris, the ultimate son of the ultimate father, reverse the
theological roles and demand self-sacrifice from his father as
penance for all the deaths; just before he reads Larry's letter

aloud, he says 'I know all about the world. I know the whole crap story. Now listen to this, and tell me what a man's got to be!' Larry is an offstage surrogate Jesus, having been, in effect, sent to his death by his father when Larry read the newspaper story. Larry has, in effect, died for the sins of Joe Keller, representing the twenty-one downed pilots. The second son is the one who must bear the burden of moral decision, always the central burden in Miller's world view. It seems unlikely that Chris will be able to follow his mother's advice: 'Don't take it on yourself', since she already knows the theological framework, despite her denial of it: 'God does not let a son be killed by his father.' Here we witness a father killed by both his sons. George, another son, also bears this burden, and Chris chastises him with, 'George, you don't want to be the voice of God, do you?' (58).

Another aspect of Chris's central role in the play is his embodiment of the theme of denial; his is a far more complex psychological portrait than Kate's protective denial or Joe's consciously defensive denial. Chris never admits to himself what he knows; it isn't until his mother confesses for Joe, even before he reads Larry's letter, that he consciously realises what his father has done. But Miller has provided significant clues throughout: why is Chris so uneasy about Joe wanting to change the name on the plant to 'Christopher Keller, Incorporated'? When Joe blusters about Steve, suspecting that he sent Ann to 'find out something', Chris retorts angrily, 'Why? What is there to find out?' When George asks for ten minutes' conversation with Joe, 'and then you'll have the answer', Chris evades the showdown. Perhaps the most damning of all the clues is Kate's saying to Jim, 'I always had the feeling that in the back of his head, Chris . . . almost knew. I didn't think it would be such a shock' (80). As George says to him, 'You know in your heart Joe did it' (60) and then adds, moments later, the heartwrenching line, 'Oh, Chris, you're a liar to yourself!' (61). This element in Chris's character calls for enormous subtlety from the actor: possessing an open face and an open nature, he must remain something of a mystery to his parents ('I'm beginning to think we don't really know him. They say in the war he was such a killer. Here he was always afraid of mice' (83). Worse, he remains a mystery to himself, as most Miller characters do. From Willy Loman in *Death of a Salesman* to Eddie Carbone in *A View from the Bridge*, from Quentin in *After the Fall* and Victor in *The Price*, to Lyman Felt in *The Ride Down Mount Morgan* – they all appear to be self-searchers but are also self-deluders. John Proctor in *The Crucible*, Miller's most powerful moral hero, may be the exception, although there are those who find his moral clarity oppressive, and sanctimonious, just as there are those who find Miller's moral clarity oppressive, and sanctimonious, as some of his protagonists even resort to suicide, and therefore self-condemnation.

Joe Keller

Miller's Everyman is both an individual and an archetype, 'a man among men' as the stage directions introduce him to us. The play demonstrates that this Everyman needs to be replaced: he is 'nearing sixty' (although in explaining his desperation to Chris he says he's sixty-one). Joe's values belong to a pre-war world, where strength was defined by physical power and making money and where loyalty was defined by caring for one's family. Note that he has no sense of loyalty to Steve, his business partner, neighbour and longtime friend, although Chris feels deep loyalty to the men he fought in the war with – loyalty that will ultimately supersede his loyalty to family. Joe's is a world where a man supports his wife and children, where he builds a legacy for his sons, and where material prosperity and conspicuous consumption are the gauge of success. Uneducated, he is not inclined to think about the world (note his wonder at the newspaper's want-ads as well as his refusal to read any news) or to introspection, and has swallowed society's values whole. Joe is a man who has not heard the Socratic dictum that the unexamined life is not worth living, and it is his tragedy to examine the moral principles by which he has lived only to discover, too late, that he has followed the wrong path.

Nevertheless, Joe's style as 'a man among men' is bluff, good-natured, and confident enough to have faced down the neighbours – his long walk down the street after he was exonerated is both hubristic and impressive – and to have won them over, so that despite their knowing he is guilty, they enjoy his company enough to play cards, to chat about what's in the newspaper, to talk and joke about families. Joe is crass and despite his white-collar success, he remains distinctly blue-collar and working-class in his manner.

His shrewd ability to handle people is clearly demonstrated when he suggests to Ann that her father could come back to work at the factory once his prison term is over; Joe is clearly trying to subvert any of their family's impulse towards revenge, and what seems like generosity is self-protection: 'I like you and George to go to your father in prison and tell him . . . "Dad, Joe wants to bring you into the business when you get out,"' Ann, 'Surprised, even shocked' replies, 'You'd have him as a partner?' Joe qualifies his offer, explaining, 'nervously', 'I want him to know that when he gets out he's got a place waitin' for him. It'll take his bitterness away. To know you got a place . . . it sweetens you' (53). Although Ann is amazed, we should recall that only a page earlier she has said, 'You're not so dumb, Joe.' Chris's rejection of Joe's notion is angry and forcible, eventually provoking Joe's outburst, 'A father is a father!' (53), a remark which seems so fraught with meaning that Joe himself is appalled.

Joe tries to explain his guilt – both to Chris and to himself – by asking that he 'see it human'. He replies to Chris's insistence that he should be in jail with the pragmatism of capitalism: 'Who worked for nothin' in the war? When they work for nothin' I'll work for nothin'. Did they ship a gun or a truck outa Detroit before they got their price?' (89).

Kate Keller
Although she seems to have the smallest role of the family, she is the paradigm of the play's deepest psychological anguish, revealing the cost of her values as well as the cost of

xl All My Sons

her repression of the truth. She is unable to grieve
straightforwardly over the death of her son and fabricates an
elaborate self-consolatory fiction by which she lives for three
years. Harold Clurman noted that 'If there is a "villain" in
the piece, it is the mother – the kindly, loving mother who
wants her brood to be safe and her home undisturbed'
('Thesis and Drama', *Lies Like Truth: Theatre Reviews and
Essays*, New York: Macmillan, 1958). Frank Rich's *New York
Times* review of the Broadway revival in 1987 calls Kate 'an
unwitting monster who destructively manipulates everyones'
guilts, enforces the most conformist social values, and
attempts, with intermittent success, to disguise psychotic
impulses as physical ailments and familiar self-martyrdom'.

We don't meet Kate until the middle of Act One when
she steps on to the porch. Miller describes her as being 'in
her early fifties, a woman of uncontrolled inspirations, and
an overwhelming capacity for love'. It is worth noting that
her dialogue in the script is ascribed to 'Mother' and,
although she is referred to by her name by the characters,
Miller clearly sees her as a maternal archetype more than as
an individual. She occupies the conventional role of mid-
twentieth-century suburban housewife, having devoted
herself to husband and children and house; one aspect of
her relationship to her husband is sarcasm; after Joe
mistakenly throws away a bag of potatoes, believing it to be
garbage, he says, 'I don't like garbage in the house.' She
replies, with tart wisdom, 'Then don't eat' (18). Chris
comments on this exchange: 'That settles you for the day',
to which Joe remarks, 'Yeah, I'm in last place again.' This
mild bickering is clearly a marital habit, and represents a
passive-aggression understandable in women whose lives are
completely defined by husbands who may strain their
loyalty and the expected wifely admiration. The garbage
exchange is also telling in that Kate is metaphorically
reminding Joe of cause and effect: there are consequences to
everything.

Miller's subtle portrayal of Kate's manipulative nature,
shows her bending the men around her – Joe, Chris,
George, Larry, Jim, Frank – to her will by making them

worry and protect her; she brings out their gallantry and eagerness to please. The younger generation, especially the unmarried Chris and George, she infantilises, reducing them to the boys they were by making them nostalgic for the innocent pleasures these battle-scarred men used to enjoy. When George appears in the middle of the play, she speaks for the America Miller indicts: 'You had big principles, Eagle Scouts the three of you; [. . .] Stop being a philosopher and look after yourself' (67). It is worth noting that the women in the play – Ann and Sue and Lydia – are not susceptible to her charm or manipulation and resist her for their own survival. These gender lines are drawn early in the play and offer a compelling picture of sexual politics at mid-century, as well as the particular pathology of a woman trapped by truths so intolerable that the only way she can deny them is by distorting her personality. How much this denial rises to the conscious surface – and how to reveal that – is the problem every actress playing Kate must solve.

Kate cannot sleep – we hear of her late nights in the back yard and the kitchen – and is, as well, tormented by disturbing dreams when she does sleep; she has headaches, which we, unlike the family, understand to be symptoms of her repressed knowledge, both of Larry's death and Joe's guilt. If she admits to herself that Larry is not coming home, that he is dead, she must also admit to herself that her husband bears some responsibility for that death. Further, if she admits her husband's guilt, she must admit her own complicity – both in keeping silent when Steve went to prison and in enjoying the material benefits of her husband's ill-gotten prosperity. Neither Chris nor Joe do anything more than merely worry about her symptoms which seems to be further indication of their own repressed knowledge and guilt. Despite looking like a 'normal' family, the Kellers are deeply troubled, a family who only seems to be 'functional'. By the end of the play, Kate's wifely loyalty shifts to maternal loyalty: no longer able to protect her husband, she must now protect her son by forgiving him: 'Don't dear. Don't take this on yourself. Forget now. Live' (91). Her sobbing is the play's final sound.

Ann Deever

Ann is introduced to us by Miller in a puzzling way: 'Ann is twenty-six, gentle but despite herself capable of holding fast to what she knows.' The implication seems to be that this wholesome, lovely woman – it is clear from everyone's reactions to seeing her again that she has grown into a beauty – is also self-assured and determined. She understands Kate's power over Chris and, with startling clarity, attempts to strike a quid pro quo deal: 'You made Chris feel guilty with me. Whether you wanted to or not, you've crippled him in front of me. I'd like you to tell him that Larry is dead and that you know it. You understand me? I'm not going out of here alone. There's no life for me that way. I want you to set him free. And then I promise you, everything will end, and we'll go away, and that's all' (84). Kate refuses Ann's terms, forcing Ann to produce Larry's suicide letter. Ann's insistence on their all knowing the truth is more for her own benefit than for any higher morality: she wants Chris for her husband and she wants him free of his mother's psychological oppression. Sue Bayliss says that Ann is 'the female version of [Chris]' (49), though her motivation is purely self-interest; it could, however, be argued that everyone in the play is similarly motivated.

When Kate reads the letter, saying, over and over, 'Oh, my God . . .', Ann's reply ('Kate, please, please . . .') is said, Miller's directions tell us, 'with pity and fear'. These emotions suggest the classic Aristotelian definition of tragedy. If Joe is the tragic figure whose death comes as a result of wisdom gained too late, then Ann's tragic emotions mirror ours; the girl next door, who is both insider and outsider, is our surrogate. Once she insists that Chris read the letter – she 'thrusts' it into his hand – she has fulfilled her dramatic role and is silent for the last intense moments of the play which belong exclusively to the family.

George Deever

George Deever is an interesting character, although the role

seems minor. George is Chris's Laertes: the foil to the
complex hero, the son whose relation to his father throws
the play's central father/son relationship into high relief.
(Note, too, that Laertes' father, Polonius, is pivotal in
Hamlet's plot just as Steve is pivotal to *All My Sons* in that
Polonius is seen to be weak and easily misled.) George's
arrival is anxiously discussed before he finally appears; we
have been keenly aware of his presence 'in the car', i.e.
offstage, as the struggle about his surprising visit continues
on stage. When he ultimately enters, Miller provides this
information: 'George is Chris's age, but a paler man, now
on the edge of his self-restraint. He speaks quietly, as though
afraid to find himself screaming' (55). Like Chris, George is
a veteran; unlike Chris, he was seriously wounded – enough
to spend a long time in hospital, and long enough to have
been studying law while recuperating. 'When I was studying
in the hospital it seemed sensible, but outside there didn't
seem to be much of a law. The trees got thick, didn't they?'
(59). Although that last sentence seems to be merely a quick
and nervous shift in subject, it is, in fact, causal: the trees
have indeed grown, enclosing the backyard, shielding the
family from the outside world. When Kate first sees him she
greets him with 'Georgie, Georgie' and with sad sympathy
takes his face in her hands and says, 'They made an old man
out of you [. . .] He looks like a ghost' (63). Significantly, she
reminds him that when he was drafted into the military she
told him, 'don't try for medals'. She insists that 'You're all
alike', implying that, like Chris (and by extension Larry),
George was too self-sacrificial. 'Relishing her solicitude', he
succumbs to her pity and maternal concern, demonstrating
once again the way the Kellers' charm has always worked.

Although we understand that brother and sister shared a
view about their father's guilt, we learn, as Ann does, that
something has radically changed George's attitude; their
joint rejection of him – not a word, not a visit, not a
Christmas card – George now sees as a 'terrible thing. We
can never be forgiven' (59). That 'terrible thing' was not
only to have abandoned him to prison, but also to have
abandoned him as family, accepting, without question, the

public view of the crime. When Chris wonders, 'The court record was good enough for you all these years, why isn't it good now? Why did you believe it all these years?', George's powerful reply, often oddly buried in the scene's commotion, is, 'Because you believed it . . . That's the truth, Chris. I believed everything, because I thought you did' (61). Thus, Chris's denial of the buried truth has caused even larger collateral damage. This also indicates the truth of what Sue Bayliss points out to Ann: Chris's charismatic idealism is dangerously persuasive.

We learn how determined Ann has been to marry Chris; not only had she told George she was going to marry Chris before Chris's proposal, even before the visit, before their first kiss, but George then felt obliged to break the years' silence and visit his father for the first time to tell him the news. Trying to imagine the motivation, there seem to have been equal parts of love and spite in his decision, just as there are in his decision to come and prevent Ann marrying Chris: he arrives demanding she collect her things and leave with him, that 'she's one item he's not going to grab. [. . .] Everything they have is covered with blood' (61).

The grim and desperate mood is broken by the arrival of Lydia with a hat she has made for Kate, whose lack of tact and sensitivity in the ensuing scene is a gauge of her crassness and her self-protectiveness: nowhere else in the play does she show how much like Joe she is. Lydia was 'Laughy' in the old days and she is repeatedly embarrassed by Kate's insistence that George should have married her; her three babies and her husband Frank having escaped the war, as well as her new womanly beauty, all make George understandably envious. Kate relentlessly pursues this theme, harping on George's seriousness with remarks like: 'Don't be so intelligent', and 'While you were getting mad about Fascism Frank was getting into her bed' (67). Despite what may well seem like Kate's cruel mockery, George succumbs to Kate's charm again, '(*laughing*). She's wonderful' (67). Part of what is so painful in this scene is the way it reveals George's nostalgia, his need for both maternal solicitude (we never learn what his relationship is with his own mother) and the ease of the past when he lived next door. Nostalgia, the longing to go back to an unrecoverable past, is an inevitable theme in a post-war play, and George embodies that theme. While Chris and Ann look forwards to a future, George, stuck in an intolerable present, looks back to a happier, more innocent past. His heartbreaking remark 'I never felt at home anywhere but here' (71) is emblematic of the hopelessness of nostalgia and the sense of alienation and anomie that marks post-war America.

Joe's approach to containing the danger George represents is to browbeat him with the past, pointing up example after example of his father's weakness. His most revealing accusation 'There are certain men in the world who rather see everybody hung before they'll take the blame' is, ironically, a self-accusation. When he accidentally reveals the lie of his 'flu' on the day of the fateful decision at the plant, George, Miller's stage directions tell us, '*stands perfectly still*' (72). The ensuing suspicion is apparently lost in Frank's arrival with Larry's horoscope, then in the cab's honking, waiting to take George to the train station. Chris and Ann seem on the verge of a showdown; George says to his sister, 'He simply told your father to kill pilots, and covered himself in bed!' Chris threateningly says, 'You'd better answer him, Annie. Answer him' (74), but this climax, too, is undermined by Kate's declaration that she has packed Ann's bag, trying to evict her from their lives. But Chris rises to Ann's defence, indignant at his mother's highhanded interference, and the moment is subsumed: 'Now get out of here, George!' George tries to pursue Ann's confrontation of the truth, and we hear their voices arguing offstage as George leaves. Unlike the main characters, George is the only one whose life is unresolved; he is, perhaps, the most modern of the play's characters: damaged, guilt-ridden, rendered aimless by his existential crisis, and exiled to a life bereft of family, friends, and meaning.

The neighbours

The Baylisses and the Lubeys serve to create a sense of neighbourhood, living as they do on either side of the Kellers' house; they also provide a spectrum of personality types, serving as foils both to each other and to the central characters. Early in Act One Frank tells Jim, 'The trouble with you is, you don't *believe* in anything', and Jim replies, 'And your trouble is that you believe in *anything*' (6). Not only do they represent distant ends of the philosophic spectrum, from optimism and credulity to pessimism and cynicism, but Frank Lubey's interest in astrology is set against Jim's medical science, which has in itself deteriorated to, as he sees it, the hand-holding of hypochondriacs.

The two couples, along with the Kellers, provide a portrait of the institution of suburban, mid-twentieth-century marriage: while Frank seems to be cheerfully married to a good-natured woman, Jim is grimly married to a sniping, unhappy woman. It's worth noting that Jim and Sue Bayliss are older than Frank and Lydia, perhaps implying that their disillusionment is yet to come. Although Kate had once thought Lydia would be George's wife, he replies, 'sadly' and with obvious regret, 'she used to laugh too much' (67) – and clearly she still does. The Lubeys' little tiff about repairing a toaster is entirely pleasant, while the Kellers' little tiff about Joe's throwing out the potatoes elicits a more biting response from Kate; and the Baylisses' about the patient on the telephone is distinctly mean-spirited.

Frank is seen as an affable, puppy-ish man, likable, but not respected or admired. His happy life may be due to his innocence as well as to good luck: he beat the draft (as a result of the year in which he was born: no wonder he is addicted to astrology), escaped the war, and got the girl. That girl, Lydia, now the mother of three children, is a 'robust, laughing girl of twenty-seven' who knew George and Ann when they were all young together. Lydia, like Ann, is literally 'the girl next door', wholesome and easily amused.

Jim's wife Sue, is a former nurse; as Joe tells her, 'You

were a nurse too long, Susie. You're too . . . too . . . realistic'
(8). Sue seems both disappointed and resentful, not only of
her husband's attitudes but at having lost her youth and
looks; when Joe tells her that Ann has arrived and that 'she's
a knockout', Sue replies sardonically, 'I should've been a
man. People are always introducing me to beautiful
women' (9).

Jim is the one of the four neighbours Miller is most
interested in: he has the largest role and, not insignificantly,
the bleakest outlook on life. No longer willing to participate
in his family (maintaining it is too hot to drive to the beach,
despite his having just driven to the station to pick up
George), he resents the compromise marriage requires; no
longer the idealistic researcher, he is now embittered and
resigned to supporting them by doing medicine of the most
pedestrian kind. His resignation gives his character the most
depth and intensity; as he tells Kate, 'I live in the usual
darkness; I can't find myself; it's even hard sometimes to
remember the kind of man I wanted to be' (80), which gives
him a profound and tragic modernity. Jim's cynicism would
be summed up years later by the American comedian
George Carlin who said, 'It's called the American dream
'cause you have to be asleep to believe it.' He also said,
'Inside every cynical person, there is a disappointed idealist',
a perfect description of Jim.

Structure

As the legendary director and critic Harold Clurman
shouted out after sitting through a rehearsal of *All My Sons'*
first production, 'Goddamit, this play is *built*!' The
architecture of a play, its structure, is what shapes the plot,
links scene to scene, works towards (or refuses to, as is the
case with some modern/contemporary plays) a decisive,
climactic event. *All My Sons* is Miller's most conventional
play structurally, and, like his early plays which immediately
followed it, *Death of a Salesman*, *The Crucible* and *A View from
the Bridge*, it raises the controversial question of the possibility

of a modern tragedy. In his 1949 essay 'Tragedy and the Common Man' (*Theatre Essays*), he argues against the Aristotelian assumption that tragedy befalls only the great; Miller wrote: 'I believe that the common man is as apt a subject for tragedy in its highest sense as kings were…I think the tragic feeling is evoked in us when we are in the presence of a character who is ready to lay down his life, if need be, to secure one thing – his sense of personal dignity…Tragedy, then, is the consequence of a man's total compulsion to evaluate himself justly.'

As regards *All My Sons,* these remarks raise the question: is Joe a tragic hero? This can, perhaps, be answered in Miller's own terms since the essay goes on to argue that, 'Tragedy enlightens – and it must, in that it points the heroic finger at the enemy of man's freedom. The thrust for freedom is the quality in tragedy which exalts. The revolutionary questioning of the stable environment is what terrifies.' That last sentence could function as a summary of *All My Sons*. Tragic dramatic structure always begins in order and disintegrates into chaos, while the comic dramatic structure begins in chaos and moves towards order, an order which acknowledges the possibility of a stable future (thus comedies often end in weddings). 'Too late' is the classic tragic lesson, and like classical tragedy, Miller's protagonist discovers what he needs to discover too late to rectify his moral error. The analysis becomes more complex if we consider that Chris – hiding from the truth of what he has known all along – is the tragic figure, rather than Joe whose error is an act of will, an incorrect moral choice. Modern thought is steeped in both psychology and sociology, and both tend to diminish the stature of the individual who, for reasons of nature or nurture, could not help doing what he did. Because Miller optimistically believes that human beings can be better than they are, he believes that life can be remediated; this is fighting drama, like Ibsen's, lacking the bleak finality of Lear's definitive 'Never, never, never, never, never.'

To trace the structure of the play, we watch the peace of Act One dented by intimations of trouble: the fallen tree,

Kate 'getting just like after [Larry] died', the arrival of Ann,
'Larry's girl' as Kate sees her, *must* see her. Each family
scene threatens to – or actually does – turn ugly until a
neighbour arrives to lighten the mood; this is a pattern
established throughout the play. There are expository
speeches built naturally into the dialogue – Ann explains
why she isn't married, Chris describes his experience in the
war and its effect on him, and, just when Chris and Ann
declare their love and kiss, George telephones to say,
mysteriously, that he will be arriving shortly, creating
suspense to carry us through the first intermission.

Act Two postpones George's arrival while Joe attempts to
assert his authority, his seeming generosity to Steve, and
thus enlist Ann as an ally; Chris's anger at Joe's willingness
to forgive Steve (entirely self-serving, but in ways we do not
know about yet), demolishes the conciliatory atmosphere.
Enter George, with 'blood in his eye', and once again the
action alternates between anger and affection, as it does
over and over again. When the showdown between Chris
and George nearly reaches its climax, Lydia arrives from
next door with the hat she has made for Kate, defusing the
tension again. The pivot of the plot appears so
inconspicuously that we barely register it as the staggering
revelation it is; George is yielding to the nostalgic tug of the
place when he says, 'I never felt at home anywhere but here
[. . .] Kate, you look so young [. . .] You too, Joe, you're
amazingly the same. The whole atmosphere is.' Joe fatefully
replies, 'Say, I ain't got time to get sick', and Kate makes a
dreadful misstep: 'He hasn't been laid up in fifteen
years . . .', to which Joe quickly replies 'Except my flu
during the war' (71). This is the inadvertent disclosure that
will bring the whole false structure of their lives crashing
down. This time Frank's bumptious entrance with Larry's
horoscope only fuels the flame, and the passionate,
heartbreaking confrontation between Joe and Chris ends
Act Two as Chris storms off. Act Three brings its own
startling revelations: Chris returns, Ann reveals Larry's
suicide letter, and Joe accepts his guilt. The structure of the
conclusion of the play is based entirely on exits.

In his Introduction to the Methuen Drama volume *Plays: One*, Miller notes that in his first produced play, *The Man Who Had All the Luck*, he had tried to write a sense of the 'amazing': 'I had tried to grasp wonder, I had tried to make it on the stage, by writing wonder' (15). After the failure of this first venture, Miller returned to that master of wonder, Dostoevsky, discovering the effectiveness of the Russian novelist's structure: 'the precise collision of inner themes during, not before or after, the high dramatic scenes'. Miller turns then to Beethoven and discovers another crucial lesson in structure: 'the holding back of climax until it was ready, the grasp of the rising line and the unwillingness to divert to an easy climax until the true one was ready. If there is one word to name the mood I felt it was *Forego*. Let nothing interfere with the shape, the direction, the intention' (16).

Acknowledging 'the shadow of Ibsen', Miller points out that 'as in Ibsen's best-known work, a great amount of time is taken up with bringing the past into the present' (20). Although he acknowledges that this kind of structuring may be out of fashion, he writes that '*All My Sons* takes its time with the past, not in deference to Ibsen's method as I saw it then, but because its theme is a question of actions and consequences, and a way had to be found to throw a long line into the past in order to make that kind of connection viable' (20). When Kate tells Ann why she's certain Larry is still alive, she says – finding the only way she can to deny a truth that is too terrible to admit – 'Because certain things have to be, and certain things can never be. Like the sun has to rise, it has to be. That's why there's God. Otherwise anything could happen. But there's God, so certain things can never happen' (29). The point, of course, is that here randomness would be a comfort: Larry's death is not meaningless but meaningful, the iron-clad logic of cause and effect; here the cause – Joe's immoral act – has created this terrible effect – Larry's suicide and the deaths of twenty-one other young men.

Finally, the structure of the play rests on Miller's vision as he expressed in *Timebends*: 'Whenever the hand of the distant past reaches out of its grave, it is always somehow absurd as well as amazing, and we tend to resist belief in it, for it seems rather magically to reveal some unreadable hidden order behind the amoral chaos of events as we rationally perceive them. But that emergence, of course, is the point of *All My Sons* – that there are times when things do indeed cohere' (135). Thus, the hints and clues about who knows what need to be fully available to us without revealing too much too soon; it is not simply a matter of our suspense, but of the characters' suspense: the connections are not merely 'between the present and the past, between events and moral consequences, [but also] between the manifest and the hidden' (*Timebends* 24).

Productions

A few key productions

1947 *All My Sons* opens on Broadway, directed by Elia Kazan

1976 Production in Jerusalem directed by Hy Kalus, starring two of Israel's leading actors, Hanna Marron as Kate and Yossi Yadin as Joe. Miller attends (in 1977) with both the President and Prime Minister of Israel, where the play has a record-breaking run.

1981 West End production in London, directed by Michael Blakemore.

2000 Production at the National Theatre, London, directed by Howard Davies (four Olivier Awards).

2002 Production at the Guthrie Theatre, Minneapolis, directed by Joe Dowling.

2008 Revival on Broadway, directed by Simon McBurrey.

Screen adaptations

1948 Universal Studios, directed by Irving Reis.

1986 American Playhouse (television), directed by Jack O'Brien.

Productions are, necessarily, interpretations of a script. The director makes choices and decisions, the actors make choices and decisions, as do the designers of the lighting, sound, and costumes. When reading a play, the reader makes all those choices, consciously or not, as we see the play happen in our mind's eye. It is crucial to read all the stage and set directions, and not to skip the italicised portions of the script eager to get on with the story.

Actors, directors, and other playwrights have much to say about Miller: for example, Patrick Stewart, the powerful British actor (who will, to some degree, always be Captain Jean-Luc Picard of *Star Trek*) said during an interview while starring in Miller's late play *The Ride Down Mount Morgan:*

> He [Miller] likes actors. Not all playwrights do, which may be surprising. But Arthur does and when I began to realize that, it's very relaxing. On numerous occasions, he said to me [sudden shift to American accent], 'I don't know how you do it! I sit there and I watch and I don't know how you do it!' [Switch back to own voice and accent] Well, that's so *charming*. [Switch back to American accent] 'I couldn't do it, it would kill me!' He likes actors, he knows that a play is not complete until it's been given flesh and blood and sometimes that flesh and blood requires that there's input from the actors and the director. (*Arthur Miller's America*, 178)

Rosemary Harris played Kate in *All My Sons*, in the 1981 production in London; it ran for a remarkable nine months at Wyndham's Theatre. She recalls:

> One of the fascinating aspects of playing Kate is the question of how much she really knows or suspects. It is a very thin line. The hope of Larry's return has to be kept alive at all costs and some of the profoundest feelings I've felt on a stage I felt during Ann's reading of Larry's suicide letter. It's hard to describe: a complete and utter emptiness engulfed by grief. I was always awfully jolly after the curtain came down but I used to wake up in the morning with a curious sense of heaviness and sorrow. After all, 'my husband' and 'my son' had killed themselves the night before. Playing Kate has been one of the joys of my theatrical life . . . I am grateful to Arthur for that character and all the people of his imagination. And I retain more than memories. All these years later I still have the costumes from that play. (*Arthur Miller and Company*, 50–1).

Making this admiration mutual, Miller told the critic Mel Gussow:

> Nobody like Rosemary Harris had ever played that part, except once, in, of all places, Jerusalem . . . She was fantastically *there*. Rosemary and Blakemore [Michael Blakemore, the production's director] didn't assume at all that the basic thing was a father and son play [. . .] with Rosemary Harris, it wasn't simply narrowed down to the conflict. She created an ambience there that you could cut with a knife. It was quite wonderful. (*Conversations with Arthur Miller*, 100–1)

The original Broadway production in 1947 won two Tony Awards: Arthur Miller for Author of Best Play and Elia Kazan for Best Direction, as well as the New York Drama Critics' Circle Award (winning over Eugene O'Neill's *The Iceman Cometh*). Brooks Atkinson, the powerful *New York Times* critic, wrote that Miller

> brings something fresh and exciting . . . Told against a single setting of an American backyard, it is a pitiless analysis of character that gathers momentum all evening and concludes with both logic and dramatic impact. Beth Merrill as the neurotic and tired mother gives us the impression of an inner strength that dominates at least one corner of the crisis. As Joe Keller, Ed Begley dramatizes the whole course of the father's poignant ordeal without losing the basic coarseness of the character. As the son, Arthur Kennedy is giving a superb performance with great power . . . [Miller is] a playwright who knows his craft and has unusual understanding of the tangled loyalties of human beings. (30 January 1947)

Miller felt that it was Atkinson's 'campaign for *All My Sons* that was responsible for its long run and my recognition as a playwright' (*Timebends*, 138).

The British production in 2000 won four Olivier Awards: Howard Davies for Best Director, William Dudley for Best Set Design, Ben Daniels for Best Supporting Actor and Julie Walters for Best Actress. In the *Independent* David Benedict wrote:

> The overwhelming passions of Julie Walters, James Hazeldine and Ben Daniels are shockingly convincing . . . At root this is a 'what did you do in the war daddy?' drama in which retribution

comes to call . . . All the five main characters fill the theatre with
tension as if holding five sticks of lit dynamite. (8 July 2000)

In the *Evening Standard* Patrick Marmion wrote:

It is an intense, immaculately conceived production packed
with compelling performances . . . Miller's writing is packed
with wit and wisdom and follows an Ibsenite dramatic
procedure of stripping away layers to reveal previously
dormant, now deepening conflicts. Not only does Howard
Davies create a vivid sense of this particular family's life, he
also creates a subliminal sense of the whole community,
illustrating the warring themes of responsibility and self-
interest. William Dudley's design, meanwhile, creates an
environment best described as wrap-around theatre. He lays a
real grass lawn, canopied with a curtain of weeping willow. To
this he adds naturalistic sounds and smells emanating from all
around the theatre. But with the stage perfectly set it is the
acting that blows you away. (7 July 2000)

In production, the design decisions most obvious and
influential to the audience are those affecting the set. The
audience can 'read a set', which is to say that the set tells
you what the play is about. The great American playwright
Edward Albee, talking about sets, observed 'It is impossible
NOT to have a set – even the total absence of a set is a set.
The only requirement is that the set be right for the
production – there are many possibilities for a play, as long
as the designer understands the play. I'm very leery of a set
that wants to tell you what the play is about – a set is a
container' (Toby Zinman, *Edward Albee*, University of
Michigan Press, 2008, 3–4). Miller's set directions, on the
other hand, describe the Kellers' back yard in minute detail,
even down to the presumed real-estate value. Miller
specifies an apple tree, although a cherry tree must have
been tempting. (American apocrypha: George Washington,
America's first president, chopped down a cherry tree when
he was a boy. When confronted by his father, he said, 'I
cannot tell a lie. I did it.') The apple tree also has its source
in Miller's life: after the stock market crash of 1929 in which
his father lost a great deal of money, the family moved to
Brooklyn, New York, and in the new back yard, Miller, then

a teenager, planted an apple tree and a pear tree; the apple tree was later knocked down in a storm. But an apple tree has unavoidable biblical associations, suggesting that the Kellers' suburban back yard is Eden, and the choice of an apple tree thus tells us what the play will be about: the loss of innocence, the acceptance of the knowledge of good and evil and thus of moral responsibility; and, further, that this pre-lapsarian world is doomed. But this is a faux Edenic world: the Kellers' fall into error happened years before the play begins, and it only remains for the denials, ignorings, and self-protective delusions to be stripped away.

Everyone *in* the play reads the apple tree as a symbol, too: for Kate the storm's wreckage signifies that it was too early to memorialise Larry's death, that it's a sign he's still alive. When she says at the start of Act Two, 'You notice there's more light with that thing gone?', we feel that she means one literal thing, while Miller means another, metaphoric, thing. When George asks about the apple-tree stump and Chris tells him, 'We had it there for Larry', George replies, 'Why, afraid you'll forget him?' It's worth noting at this point that *Timebends* ends with Miller's evocative declaration: 'the truth, the first truth, probably, is that we are all connected, watching one another. Even the trees.' Miller's 'secluded atmosphere' is created by 'closely planted poplars', trees that, we will learn, have grown taller and denser over the years, and thus symbolically as well literally seclude the back yard even more. Seclusion, of course, keeps in, imprisoning, as well as keeping out, protecting and isolating.

Historically, Miller's directions for this play invited the most realistic of sets, but almost always the realism is laced with symbolism. The original set was designed by Mordecai Gorelik for the 1947 Broadway premiere; Gorelik organised his sets, as Miller explains in *Timebends*, 'around a metaphoric statement condensing the central image of the play'. He had designed a back yard with a bump, and Miller worried the actors would fall over it. 'What's the point of it, Max – a rise like that in the middle of the stage?' The reply was, 'You have written a graveyard play and not some factual report. The play is taking place in a cemetery where their son is buried, and he is also their buried conscience reaching up to them out of the earth. Even if it inconveniences them [the actors] it will keep reminding them what the hell all this acting is really *about*. The bump stays!' (275).

Looking at photographs of a dozen productions reveals that they are all remarkably and interestingly similar: the same back yard, the same wooden lawn furniture, the same fretworked gazebo. There have been productions where the back yard was picket-fenced, as though to signify the bars of a prison, picking up Joe's ongoing game with the neighbourhood boys who believe there's a jail in the house, as well as implying the real prison Steve is in and Joe should be in. The possibilities for easy symbolism are all remarkably similar.

John Lee Beatty, the pre-eminent set designer, acknowledged that his inspiration for the 2002 Guthrie production in Minneapolis was the Grant Wood painting *American Gothic*; what he hoped to achieve was an 'ironic twist', wanting it to seem 'attractive and yet, oddly, a little bit off, not quite realistic'. Beatty noted that 'underlying that painting and through his other work, [Wood] explores solid philosophical and aesthetic backgrounds having to do with American identity. His idyllic images of America are rendered through a potently ironic perspective.' In his comments to his actors and staff early in the rehearsal process, Beatty quoted Miller saying that 'nothing should interfere with its artifice'. His interpretation aimed to avoid the 'nostalgically naturalistic'.

The American playwright John Guare recalls an uproarious lunch with Miller:

> I told Arthur how my feelings about him as a writer had changed. I had at one time thought him the enemy, consigned to the poetry-free pits of naturalism Hell. Not until I saw *The American Clock* did I realise how shot through to its very bones the play was with surrealistic imagery and that this surrealism was indeed responsible for that which was most powerful about the play. I subsequently saw a conventional revival of *All My Sons*. I closed my eyes and simply listened to the play's madness and realized one day some visionary director will find

a way to liberate Arthur's plays from their cage of traditional
psychological realism. (*Arthur Miller and Company*, 223)

Simon McBurney would be that director. His production
opened on Broadway in 2008. He was the least likely
director for this American classic, being both British and
wildly experimental (he is the artistic director of the anti-
realist company Complicite). McBurney was asked by
Rebecca Miller, Arthur Miller's daughter, to direct *All My
Sons*, and he remembers Arthur Miller telling him in 2001,
'In America I've always felt that people have either tried to
honor it [the play] too much to the letter or there has been
this heavy hand of naturalism on it, and nothing has been
taken to the hilt.' As a *New York Times* interview noted, there
is no better guide to the hilt than McBurney who said that
rather than adding to the play, he wanted to strip it down,
which turned out to mean removing the written set
directions. In Tom Pye's set design there were no wings
where actors could hide in order to preserve the realistic
illusion on stage, no poplar trees, and not even a house: the
upstage wall was an immense weathered wood construction,
dwarfing the actors, with one small window set eerily far
above the normal height of an upstairs room.

The production made other intrusions on the naturalistic
perspective: Keller (played by John Lithgow) enters the stage
carrying the playbook from which he reads the opening stage
directions; a free-standing screen door signified entering and
leaving the house; a pay-phone was stuck on to the
proscenium arch; and huge cinematic projections punctuated
the action with memories and highlighted historical context.
The result was not a back yard, but a stage.

McBurney began the play earlier than Miller does: the tree
is still standing, the storm occurs, Kate comes out in her robe,
reaching up to the heavens, and the tree is knocked over. At
the National Theatre in London in 2000, Howard Davies's
directorial choice began the play with Kate watching the
lightning strike the apple tree. McBurney, like Miller, but
unlike Davies, does not seem to want to shift the burden of
responsibility to the cosmos; his inclination is, like Miller's, far
more on the human, the psychological, and the ethical.

Dismantling the furniture of realism yielded surprising meaning, making this play both more interesting – which is to say less moralistic – and more clearly and persuasively connected to the vision and the style of Miller's late plays: *The Ride Down Mount Morgan*, *Resurrection Blues*, and *Mr Peters' Connections*. This is a valuable kind of rereading, starting from the end and looking backwards. *All My Sons* battles through the human tug-of-war between destiny and free will – the human question inherent in the myth of Eden, and thus fundamental to Western culture – and this production emphasised that battle. And as the Edenic drama in Genesis shows us, the hardest thing for human beings is to take responsibility for our actions. The Judeo-Christian implications of *All My Sons* are immense, but if we read this production set, we feel what McBurney, interpreting Miller, wanted us to feel. McBurney said that: 'Miller is creating a modern American tragedy here . . . it's attempting to find the explosive animal questions of humanity in the play, which of course are the questions at the heart of Greek drama' (*American Theatre*, December 2008, pp. 88–9). A case made, in this instance, partly by the set design.

Rebecca Miller said of the McBurney production: 'the raw power of the play has never been unleashed in this way . . . It is the purest manifestation of the play I can imagine. I hope this will open the door to more extraordinary, unexpected productions of Miller plays' (*American Theatre*, December 2008).

The films

The first film version makes every Hollywood mistake in adapting a successful play to the screen. Directed by Irving Reis in 1948 and rewritten by the producer, Chester Erskine, the film 'opens up' the play to many settings; we go inside the house, out to dinner at the shore restaurant, to the Keller factory, to the prison to hear Steve's actual version of the fateful day (his name is changed to Herb), and on a romantic, moonlit drive. This undermines the effect of imprisonment of the play's single set and the significance of the hedged-in back yard. Further, almost all the ambiguities of character stemming from denial have been erased, and the motivations, by being flattened out, make much less sense, all, apparently, in the interests of making the moral lesson overly explicit. For example: Chris tells Joe, 'If it turned out you weren't telling the truth, I'd kill you', which is a far different and less persuasive foreshadowing of the conclusion than Joe's line in the play, 'I'm his father and he's my son, and if there's something bigger than that I'll put a bullet in my head.'

Edward G. Robinson's Joe is grim and self-important; he is particularly unlikable at the poker game, where he treats people like lackeys, wins everyone's money and gloats, although this behaviour seems to win everyone's admiration, including Chris's. The film's old-fashioned mores startle, especially Joe kissing Ann on the lips. Burt Lancaster as Chris is earnest throughout, never suspicious, always eager to please his parents; his face registers little emotion. All the war stories and the resentment he feels about post-war America have been erased from the screenplay. Like Chris, Ann seems to lack a vivid personality, providing only for the requirements of the plot.

Kate was Mady Christians' last film performance, and her Austrian accent and Germanic hairdo lend the role an unsettling old-time movie-villain quality. We see her eavesdrop (accompanied by spooky music) on Ann's phone conversation with George (Howard Duff), and her affection seems too blatantly predatory and cloying. The Baylisses have been transformed into a high-spirited, sexy couple.

The 1986 made-for-television film is, on the other hand, faithful to Miller's script. Under Jack O'Brien's strong direction, the actors find every nuance within a vivid naturalistic style. Filmed in unobtrusive colour, acknowledging the breaks between acts, this production is passionate and deeply moving. Aiden Quinn (as Chris), James Whitmore (as Joe), Michael Learned (as Kate), Joan Allen (as Ann), and Zeljko Ivanek (as George) all turn in impressive performances.

Further Reading

Works by Arthur Miller

Arthur Miller Plays. 6 vols. London: Methuen, 1988–2009 (vol. 1:
   *All My Sons, Death of a Salesman, The Crucible, A Memory of Two
   Mondays, A View from the Bridge*; vol. 2: *The Misfits, After the Fall,
   Incident at Vichy, The Price, Creation of the World, Playing for Time*;
   vol. 3: *The American Clock, The Archbishop's Ceiling, Two-Way
   Mirror*; vol. 4: *The Golden Years, The Man Who Had All the Luck, I
   Can't Remember Anything, Clara*; vol. 5: *The Last Yankee, The Ride
   Down Mount Morgan, Almost Everybody Wins*; vol. 6: *Broken Glass,
   Mr Peters' Connections, Resurrection Blues, Finishing the Picture*). Vol.
   1 contains a valuable introduction by Miller, including his
   discussion of *All My Sons*.
A View from the Bridge, with commentary and notes by Stephen
   Marino. London: Methuen Drama, 2010
The Crucible, with commentary and notes by Susan C.W.
   Abbotson. London: Methuen Drama, 2010
Death of a Salesman, with commentary and notes by Enoch Brater.
   London: Methuen Drama, 2010
Echoes Down the Corridor, ed. Steven R. Centola, London:
   Methuen, 2000. Collected essays 1944–2000.
'*Salesman' in Beijing*. London: Methuen, 1984. About Miller's
   experience of working on a production of *Death of a Salesman* in
   China, underscoring the universality of Miller's themes.
   Photographs by Miller's wife, Inge Morath.
The Theatre Essays of Arthur Miller, Robert A. Martin. 2nd edn
   London: Methuen, 1994
Timebends: A Life. Autobiography/memoir. London: Methuen, 1987

About Miller and his works

Bigsby, Christopher, ed. *Arthur Miller and Company*. London
   Methuen, 1990. A collection of brief comments by actors,

playwrights, directors, reviewers, and designers about working on Miller's plays.

Bigsby, C.W.E. *Arthur Miller: 1915–1962.* The most recent biography, focusing on the political issues in Miller's life, stopping four decades before his death. London: Weidenfeld and Nicolson 2009

Bigsby, C.W.E., ed. *The Cambridge Companion to Arthur Miller.* Cambridge: Cambridge University Press, 1997. A collection of scholarly essays.

Brater, Enoch. *Arthur Miller: A Playwright's Life and Works.* London: Thames & Hudson, 2005. Includes excellent photographs.

Brater, Enoch, ed. *Arthur Miller's America: Theater and Culture in a Time of Change.* Ann Arbor: University of Michigan Press, 2004. A collection of essays by critics, scholars and theatre practitioners on the occasion of Miller's eighty-fifth birthday; includes valuable commentary on the late plays.

Brater, Enoch, ed. *Arthur Miller's Global Theater.* Ann Arbor: University of Michigan Press, 2007. A collection of essays about productions of Miller's plays around the world written by international scholars.

Centola, Steven R. *The Achievement of Arthur Miller: New Essays.* Dallas: Contemporary Research Associates, 1995.

Denison, Patricia D. '*All My Sons*: Competing Contexts and Comparative Scales' in *Arthur Miller's America: Theater and Culture in a Time of Change,* ed. Enoch Brater. Ann Arbor: University of Michigan Press, 2004, 46–59. Ann examination of the play focused on social context and referencing various productions.

Ferres, John H. *Arthur Miller: A Reference Guide.* Boston: G.K.Hall, 1979. A comprehensive list of material available up to 1978, arranged in chronological order.

Goldstein, Laurence, ed. *Michigan Quarterly Review: Special Issue: Arthur Miller.* Ann Arbor: University of Michigan Press, 1998. A collection of commemorative essays, panel discussion transcripts, poems, appreciations, and reminiscences contributed by major scholars and playwrights.

Haedicke, Susan. 'Arthur Miller: A Bibliographic Essay' in *The Cambridge Companion to Arthur Miller,* ed. C.W.E. Bigsby. Cambridge: Cambridge University Press, 1997, 245–66. An

excellent and exhaustive bibliography, arranged by subject
(i.e. 'theatrical perspective', 'psychology').

Roudané, Matthew and Arthur Miller. *Conversations with Arthur Miller*. Jackson and London: University Press of Mississippi, 1987. A collection of useful interviews.

Zeifman, Hersh. '*All My Sons After the Fall*: Arthur Miller and the Rage for Order' in *The Theatrical Gamut: Notes for a Post-Beckettian Stage*, ed. Enoch Brater. Ann Arbor: University of Michigan Press, 1995. An illuminating essay linking the two plays in surprising and persuasive ways.

All My Sons

A Play in Three Acts

Characters

Joe Keller
Kate Keller
Chris Keller
Ann Deever
George Deever
Dr Jim Bayliss
Sue Bayliss
Frank Lubey
Lydia Lubey
Bert

Act One

The back yard of the **Keller** *home in the outskirts of an American town. August of our era.*

The stage is hedged on right and left by tall, closely planted poplars which lend the yard a secluded atmosphere. Upstage is filled with the back of the house and its open, unroofed porch which extends into the yard some six feet. The house is two stories high and has seven rooms. It would have cost perhaps fifteen thousand in the early twenties when it was built. Now it is nicely painted, looks tight and comfortable, and the yard is green with sod, here and there plants whose season is gone. At the right, beside the house, the entrance of the driveway can be seen, but the poplars cut off view of its continuation downstage. In the left corner, downstage, stands the four-foot-high stump of a slender apple tree whose upper trunk and branches lie toppled beside it, fruit still clinging to its branches.

Downstage right is a small, trellised arbor, shaped like a sea shell, with a decorative bulb hanging from its forward-curving roof. Garden chairs and a table are scattered about. A garbage pail on the ground next to the porch steps, a wire leaf-burner near it.

On the rise: It is early Sunday morning. **Joe Keller** *is sitting in the sun reading the want ads of the Sunday paper, the other sections of which lie neatly on the ground beside him. Behind his back, inside the arbor,* **Doctor Jim Bayliss** *is reading part of the paper at the table.*

Keller *is nearing sixty. A heavy man of stolid mind and build, a business man these many years, but with the imprint of the machine-shop worker and boss still upon him. When he reads, when he speaks, when he listens, it is with the terrible concentration of the uneducated man for whom there is still wonder in many commonly known things, a man whose judgments must be dredged out of experience and a peasant-like common sense. A man among men.*

Doctor Bayliss *is nearly forty. A wry self-controlled man, an easy talker, but with a wisp of sadness that clings even to his self-effacing humor.*

At curtain, **Jim** *is standing at left, staring at the broken tree. He taps a pipe on it, blows through the pipe, feels in his pockets for tobacco, then speaks.*

Jim   Where's your tobacco?

Keller   I think I left it on the table. (**Jim** *goes slowly to table in the arbor, finds a pouch, and sits there on the bench, filling his pipe.*) Gonna rain tonight.

Jim   Paper says so?

Keller   Yeah, right here.

Jim   Then it can't rain.

Frank Lubey *enters, through a small space between the poplars.* **Frank** *is thirty-two but balding. A pleasant, opinionated man, uncertain of himself, with a tendency toward peevishness when crossed, but always wanting it pleasant and neighborly. He rather saunters in, leisurely, nothing to do. He does not notice* **Jim** *in the arbor. On his greeting,* **Jim** *does not bother looking up.*

Frank   Hya.

Keller   Hello, Frank. What's doin'?

Frank   Nothin'. Walking off my breakfast. (*Looks up at the sky.*) That beautiful? Not a cloud.

Keller (*looking up*)   Yeah, nice.

Frank   Every Sunday ought to be like this.

Keller (*indicating the sections beside him*)   Want the paper?

Frank   What's the difference, it's all bad news. What's today's calamity?

Keller   I don't know, I don't read the news part any more. It's more interesting in the want ads.

Frank   Why, you trying to buy something?

Keller   No, I'm just interested. To see what people want, y'know? For instance, here's a guy is lookin' for two Newfoundland dogs. Now what's he want with two Newfoundland dogs?

Frank   That is funny.

Keller   Here's another one. Wanted – old dictionaries. High prices paid. Now what's a man going to do with an old dictionary?

Frank   Why not? Probably a book collector.

Keller   You mean he'll make a living out of that?

Frank   Sure, there's a lot of them.

Keller (*shaking his head*)   All the kind of business goin' on. In my day, either you were a lawyer, or a doctor, or you worked in a shop. Now –

Frank   Well, I was going to be a forester once.

Keller   Well, that shows you; in my day, there was no such thing. (*Scanning the page, sweeping it with his hand.*) You look at a page like this you realize how ignorant you are. (*Softly, with wonder, as he scans page.*) Psss!

Frank (*noticing tree*)   Hey, what happened to your tree?

Keller   Ain't that awful? The wind must've got it last night. You heard the wind, didn't you?

Frank   Yeah, I got a mess in my yard, too. (*Goes to tree.*) What a pity. (*Turning to* **Keller**.) What'd Kate say?

Keller   They're all asleep yet. I'm just waiting for her to see it.

Frank (*struck*)   You know? – it's funny.

Keller   What?

Frank   Larry was born in August. He'd been twenty-seven this month. And his tree blows down.

Keller (*touched*)   I'm surprised you remember his birthday, Frank. That's nice.

Frank   Well, I'm working on his horoscope.

Keller   How can you make him a horoscope? That's for the future, ain't it?

Frank Well, what I'm doing is this, see. Larry was reported missing on November twenty-fifth, right?

Keller Yeah?

Frank Well, then, we assume that if he was killed it was on November twenty-fifth. Now, what Kate wants –

Keller Oh, Kate asked you to make a horoscope?

Frank Yeah, what she wants to find out is whether November twenty-fifth was a favorable day for Larry.

Keller What is that, favorable day?

Frank Well, a favorable day for a person is a fortunate day, according to his stars. In other words it would be practically impossible for him to have died on his favorable day.

Keller Well, was that his favorable day? – November twenty-fifth?

Frank That's what I'm working on to find out. It takes time! See, the point is, if November twenty-fifth was his favorable day, then it's completely possible he's alive somewhere, because – I mean it's possible. (*He notices* **Jim** *now.* **Jim** *is looking at him as though at an idiot. To* **Jim** *– with an uncertain laugh.*) I didn't even see you.

Keller (*to* **Jim**) Is he talkin' sense?

Jim Him? He's all right. He's just completely out of his mind, that's all.

Frank (*peeved*) The trouble with you is, you don't *believe* in anything.

Jim And your trouble is that you believe in *anything*. You didn't see my kid this morning, did you?

Frank No.

Keller Imagine? He walked off with his thermometer. Right out of his bag.

Jim (*getting up*) What a problem. One look at a girl and he takes her temperature. (*Goes to driveway, looks upstage toward street.*)

Frank That boy's going to be a real doctor; he's smart.

Jim Over my dead body he'll be a doctor. A good beginning, too.

Frank Why? It's an honorable profession.

Jim (*looking at him tiredly*) Frank, will you stop talking like a civics book? (**Keller** *laughs.*)

Frank Why, I saw a movie a couple of weeks ago, reminded me of you. There was a doctor in that picture –

Keller Don Ameche!

Frank I think it was, yeah. And he worked in his basement discovering things. That's what you ought to do; you could help humanity, instead of –

Jim I would love to help humanity on a Warner Brothers salary.

Keller (*pointing at him, laughing*) That's very good, Jim.

Jim (*looking toward house*) Well, where's the beautiful girl was supposed to be here?

Frank (*excited*) Annie came?

Keller Sure, sleepin' upstairs. We picked her up on the one o'clock train last night. Wonderful thing. Girl leaves here, a scrawny kid. Couple of years go by, she's a regular woman. Hardly recognized her, and she was running in and out of this yard all her life. That was a very happy family used to live in your house, Jim.

Jim Like to meet her. The block can use a pretty girl. In the whole neighborhood there's not a damned thing to look at. (**Sue**, **Jim**'s wife, enters. *She is rounding forty, an overweight woman who fears it. On seeing her* **Jim** *wryly adds:*) Except my wife, of course.

Sue (*in same spirit*) Mrs Adams is on the phone, you dog.

Jim (*to* **Keller**) Such is the condition which prevails – (*Going to his wife.*) My love, my light.

Sue Don't sniff around me. (*Pointing to their house.*) And give her a nasty answer. I can smell her perfume over the phone.

Jim What's the matter with her now?

Sue I don't know, dear. She sounds like she's in terrible pain – unless her mouth is full of candy.

Jim Why don't you just tell her to lay down?

Sue She enjoys it more when you tell her to lay down. And when are you going to see Mr Hubbard?

Jim My dear; Mr Hubbard is not sick, and I have better things to do than to sit there and hold his hand.

Sue It seems to me that for ten dollars you could hold his hand.

Jim (*to* **Keller**) If your son wants to play golf tell him I'm ready. Or if he'd like to take a trip around the world for about thirty years. (*He exits.*)

Keller Why do you needle him? He's a doctor, women are supposed to call him up.

Sue All I said was Mrs Adams is on the phone. Can I have some of your parsley?

Keller Yeah, sure. (*She goes to parsley box and pulls some parsley.*) You were a nurse too long, Susie. You're too . . . too . . . realistic.

Sue (*laughing, pointing at him*) Now you said it!

Lydia Lubey *enters. She is a robust, laughing girl of twenty-seven.*

Lydia Frank, the toaster – (*Sees the others.*) Hya.

Keller Hello!

Lydia (*to* **Frank**) The toaster is off again.

Frank Well, plug it in, I just fixed it.

Lydia (*kindly, but insistently*)   Please, dear, fix it back like it was before.

Frank   I don't know why you can't learn to turn on a simple thing like a toaster! (*He exits.*)

Sue (*laughing*)   Thomas Edison.

Lydia (*apologetically*)   He's really very handy. (*She sees broken tree.*) Oh, did the wind get your tree?

Keller   Yeah, last night.

Lydia   Oh, what a pity. Annie get in?

Keller   She'll be down soon. Wait'll you meet her, Sue, she's a knockout.

Sue   I should've been a man. People are always introducing me to beautiful women. (*To* **Joe**.) Tell her to come over later: I imagine she'd like to see what we did with her house. And thanks. (*She exits.*)

Lydia   Is she still unhappy, Joe?

Keller   Annie? I don't suppose she goes around dancing on her toes, but she seems to be over it.

Lydia   She going to get married? Is there anybody – ?

Keller   I suppose – say, it's a couple years already. She can't mourn a boy forever.

Lydia   It's so strange – Annie's here and not even married. And I've got three babies. I always thought it'd be the other way around.

Keller   Well, that's what a war does. I had two sons, now I got one. It changed all the tallies. In my day when you had sons it was an honor. Today a doctor could make a million dollars if he could figure out a way to bring a boy into the world without a trigger finger.

Lydia   You know, I was just reading –

Enter **Chris Keller** *from house, stands in doorway.*

Lydia   Hya, Chris.

Frank *shouts from offstage.*

Frank   Lydia, come in here! If you want the toaster to work don't plug in the malted mixer.

Lydia (*embarrassed, laughing*)   Did I?

Frank   And the next time I fix something don't tell me I'm crazy! Now come in here!

Lydia (*to* **Keller**)   I'll never hear the end of this one.

Keller (*calling to* **Frank**)   So what's the difference? Instead of toast have a malted!

Lydia   Sh! sh! (*She exits, laughing.*)

Chris *watches her off. He is thirty-two; like his father, solidly built, a listener. A man capable of immense affection and loyalty. He has a cup of coffee in one hand, part of a doughnut in the other.*

Keller   You want the paper?

Chris   That's all right, just the book section. (*He bends down and pulls out part of paper on porch floor.*)

Keller   You're always reading the book section and you never buy a book.

Chris (*coming down to settee*)   I like to keep abreast of my ignorance. (*He sits on settee.*)

Keller   What is that, every week a new book comes out?

Chris   Lot of new books.

Keller   All different.

Chris   All different.

Keller *shakes his head, puts knife down on bench, takes oilstone up to the cabinet.*

Keller   Psss! Annie up yet?

Chris   Mother's giving her breakfast in the dining room.

Keller (*looking at broken tree*)   See what happened to the tree?

Chris (*without looking up*)   Yeah.

Keller   What's Mother going to say?

Bert *runs on from driveway. He is about eight. He jumps on stool, then on* **Keller**'s *back.*

Bert   You're finally up.

Keller (*swinging him around and putting him down*)   Ha! Bert's here! Where's Tommy? He's got his father's thermometer again.

Bert   He's taking a reading.

Chris   What!

Bert   But it's only oral.

Keller   Oh, well, there's no harm in oral. So what's new this morning, Bert?

Bert   Nothin'. (*He goes to broken tree, walks around it.*)

Keller   Then you couldn't've made a complete inspection of the block. In the beginning, when I first made you a policeman you used to come in every morning with something new. Now, nothin's ever new.

Bert   Except some kids from Thirtieth Street. They started kicking a can down the block, and I made them go away because you were sleeping.

Keller   Now you're talkin', Bert. Now you're on the ball. First thing you know I'm liable to make you a detective.

Bert (*pulling him down by the lapel and whispering in his ear*)   Can I see the jail now?

Keller   Seein' the jail ain't allowed, Bert. You know that.

Bert   Aw, I betcha there isn't even a jail. I don't see any bars on the cellar windows.

Keller   Bert, on my word of honor there's a jail in the basement. I showed you my gun, didn't I?

Bert   But that's a hunting gun.

Keller   That's an arresting gun!

Bert   Then why don't you ever arrest anybody? Tommy said another dirty word to Doris yesterday, and you didn't even demote him.

Keller *chuckles and winks at* **Chris**, *who is enjoying all this.*

Keller   Yeah, that's a dangerous character, that Tommy. (*Beckons him closer.*) What word does he say?

Bert (*backing away quickly in great embarrassment*)   Oh, I can't say that.

Keller (*grabbing him by the shirt and pulling him back*)   Well, gimme an idea.

Bert   I can't. It's not a nice word.

Keller   Just whisper it in my ear. I'll close my eyes. Maybe I won't even hear it.

Bert, *on tiptoe, puts his lips to* **Keller**'s *ear, then in unbearable embarrassment steps back.*

Bert   I can't, Mr Keller.

Chris (*laughing*)   Don't make him do that.

Keller   Okay, Bert. I take your word. Now go out, and keep both eyes peeled.

Bert (*interested*)   For what?

Keller   For what! Bert, the whole neighborhood is depending on you. A policeman don't ask questions. Now peel them eyes!

Bert (*mystified, but willing*)   Okay. (*He runs offstage back of arbor.*)

Keller (*calling after him*)   And mum's the word, Bert.

Bert *stops and sticks his head through the arbor.*

Bert   About what?

Keller   Just in general. Be v-e-r-y careful.

Bert (*nodding in bewilderment*)   Okay. (*He exits.*)

Keller (*laughing*)   I got all the kids crazy!

Chris   One of these days, they'll all come in here and beat your brains out.

Keller   What's she going to say? Maybe we ought to tell her before she sees it.

Chris   She saw it.

Keller   How could she see it? I was the first one up. She was still in bed.

Chris   She was out here when it broke.

Keller   When?

Chris   About four this morning. (*Indicating window above them.*) I heard it cracking and I woke up and looked out. She was standing right here when it cracked.

Keller   What was she doing out here four in the morning?

Chris   I don't know. When it cracked she ran back into the house and cried in the kitchen.

Keller   Did you talk to her?

Chris   No, I – I figured the best thing was to leave her alone. (*Pause.*)

Keller (*deeply touched*)   She cried hard?

Chris   I could hear her right through the floor of my room.

Keller (*after slight pause*)   What was she doing out here at that hour? (**Chris** *silent. With an undertone of anger showing:*) She's dreaming about him again. She's walking around at night.

Chris   I guess she is.

Keller   She's getting just like after he died. (*Slight pause.*) What's the meaning of that?

Chris I don't know the meaning of it. (*Slight pause.*) But I know one thing, Dad. We've made a terrible mistake with Mother.

Keller What?

Chris Being dishonest with her. That kind of thing always pays off, and now it's paying off.

Keller What do you mean, dishonest?

Chris You know Larry's not coming back and I know it. Why do we allow her to go on thinking that we believe with her?

Keller What do you want to do, argue with her?

Chris I don't want to argue with her, but it's time she realized that nobody believes Larry is alive any more. (**Keller** *simply moves away, thinking, looking at the ground.*) Why shouldn't she dream of him, walk the nights waiting for him? Do we contradict her? Do we say straight out that we have no hope any more? That we haven't had any hope for years now?

Keller (*frightened at the thought*) You can't say that to her.

Chris We've got to say it to her.

Keller How're you going to prove it? Can you prove it?

Chris For God's sake, three years! Nobody comes back after three years. It's insane.

Keller To you it is, and to me. But not to her. You can talk yourself blue in the face, but there's no body and there's no grave, so where are you?

Chris Sit down, Dad. I want to talk to you.

Keller *looks at him searchingly a moment.*

Keller The trouble is the goddam newspapers. Every month some boy turns up from nowhere, so the next one is going to be Larry, so –

Chris All right, all right, listen to me. (*Slight pause.* **Keller** *sits on settee.*) You know why I asked Annie here, don't you?

Keller (*he knows, but –*)   Why?

Chris You know.

Keller Well, I got an idea, but – What's the story?

Chris I'm going to ask her to marry me. (*Slight pause.*)

Keller *nods.*

Keller Well, that's only your business, Chris.

Chris You know it's not only my business.

Keller What do you want me to do? You're old enough to know your own mind.

Chris (*asking, annoyed*)   Then it's all right, I'll go ahead with it?

Keller Well, you want to be sure Mother isn't going to –

Chris Then it isn't just my business.

Keller I'm just sayin' –

Chris Sometimes you infuriate me, you know that? Isn't it your business, too, if I tell this to Mother and she throws a fit about it? You have such a talent for ignoring things.

Keller I ignore what I gotta ignore. The girl is Larry's girl.

Chris She's not Larry's girl.

Keller From Mother's point of view he is not dead and you have no right to take his girl. (*Slight pause.*) Now you can go on from there if you know where to go, but I'm tellin' you I don't know where to go. See? I don't know. Now what can I do for you?

Chris I don't know why it is, but every time I reach out for something I want, I have to pull back because other people will suffer. My whole bloody life, time after time after time.

Keller You're a considerate fella, there's nothing wrong in that.

Chris   To hell with that.

Keller   Did you ask Annie yet?

Chris   I wanted to get this settled first.

Keller   How do you know she'll marry you? Maybe she feels the same way Mother does?

Chris   Well, if she does, then that's the end of it. From her letters I think she's forgotten him. I'll find out. And then we'll thrash it out with Mother? Right? Dad, don't avoid me.

Keller   The trouble is, you don't see enough women. You never did.

Chris   So what? I'm not fast with women.

Keller   I don't see why it has to be Annie.

Chris   Because it is.

Keller   That's a good answer, but it don't answer anything. You haven't seen her since you went to war. It's five years.

Chris   I can't help it. I know her best. I was brought up next door to her. These years when I think of someone for my wife, I think of Annie. What do you want, a diagram?

Keller   I don't want a diagram . . . I – I'm – She thinks he's coming back, Chris. You marry that girl and you're pronouncing him dead. Now what's going to happen to Mother? Do you know? I don't! (*Pause.*)

Chris   All right, then, Dad.

Keller (*thinking* **Chris** *has retreated*)   Give it some more thought.

Chris   I've given it three years of thought. I'd hoped that if I waited, Mother would forget Larry and then we'd have a regular wedding and everything happy. But if that can't happen here, then I'll have to get out.

Keller   What the hell is *this*?

Chris   I'll get out. I'll get married and live some place else. Maybe in New York.

Keller   Are you crazy?

Chris   I've been a good son too long, a good sucker. I'm through with it.

Keller   You've got a business here, what the hell is this?

Chris   The business! The business doesn't inspire me.

Keller   Must you be inspired?

Chris   Yes. I like it an hour a day. If I have to grub for money all day long at least at evening I want it beautiful. I want a family, I want some kids, I want to build something I can give myself to. Annie is in the middle of that. Now . . . where do I find it?

Keller   You mean – (*Goes to him.*) Tell me something, you mean you'd leave the business?

Chris   Yes. On this I would.

Keller (*after a pause*)   Well . . . you don't want to think like that.

Chris   Then help me stay here.

Keller   All right, but – but don't think like that. Because what the hell did I work for? That's only for you, Chris, the whole shootin' match is for you!

Chris   I know that, Dad. Just you help me stay here.

Keller (*putting a fist up to* **Chris***'s jaw*)   But don't think that way, you hear me?

Chris   I am thinking that way.

Keller (*lowering his hand*)   I don't understand you, do I?

Chris   No, you don't. I'm a pretty tough guy.

Keller   Yeah. I can see that.

Mother *appears on porch. She is in her early fifties, a woman of uncontrolled inspirations and an overwhelming capacity for love.*

Mother   Joe?

Chris (*going toward porch*)   Hello, Mom.

Mother (*indicating house behind her; to* **Keller**)   Did you take a bag from under the sink?

Keller   Yeah, I put it in the pail.

Mother   Well, get it out of the pail. That's my potatoes.

Chris *bursts out laughing – goes up into alley.*

Keller (*laughing*)   I thought it was garbage.

Mother   Will you do me a favor, Joe? Don't be helpful.

Keller   I can afford another bag of potatoes.

Mother   Minnie scoured that pail in boiling water last night. It's cleaner than your teeth.

Keller   And I don't understand why, after I worked forty years and I got a maid, why I have to take out the garbage.

Mother   If you would make up your mind that every bag in the kitchen isn't full of garbage you wouldn't be throwing out my vegetables. Last time it was the onions.

Chris *comes on, hands her bag.*

Keller   I don't like garbage in the house.

Mother   Then don't eat. (*She goes into the kitchen with bag.*)

Chris   That settles you for today.

Keller   Yeah, I'm in last place again. I don't know, once upon a time I used to think that when I got money again I would have a maid and my wife would take it easy. Now I got money, and I got a maid, and my wife is workin' for the maid. (*He sits in one of the chairs.*)

Mother *comes out on last line. She carries a pot of string beans.*

Mother   It's her day off, what are you crabbing about?

Chris (*to* **Mother**)   Isn't Annie finished eating?

Mother (*looking around preoccupiedly at yard*)   She'll be right out. (*Moves.*) That wind did some job on this place. (*Of the tree.*) So much for that, thank God.

Keller (*indicating chair beside him*)   Sit down, take it easy.

Mother (*pressing her hand to top of her head*)   I've got such a funny pain on the top of my head.

Chris   Can I get you an aspirin?

Mother *picks a few petals off ground, stands there smelling them in her hand, then sprinkles them over plants.*

Mother   No more roses. It's so funny . . . everything decides to happen at the same time. This month is his birthday; his tree blows down, Annie comes. Everything that happened seems to be coming back. I was just down the cellar, and what do I stumble over? His baseball glove. I haven't seen it in a century.

Chris   Don't you think Annie looks well?

Mother   Fine. There's no question about it. She's a beauty . . . I still don't know what brought her here. Not that I'm not glad to see her, but –

Chris   I just thought we'd all like to see each other again. (**Mother** *just looks at him, nodding ever so slightly – almost as though admitting something.*) And I wanted to see her myself.

Mother (*as her nods halt, to* **Keller**)   The only thing is I think her nose got longer. But I'll always love that girl. She's one that didn't jump into bed with somebody else as soon as it happened with her fella.

Keller (*as though that were impossible for* **Annie**)   Oh, what're you – ?

Mother   Never mind. Most of them didn't wait till the telegrams were opened. I'm just glad she came, so you can see

I'm not *completely* out of my mind. (*Sits, and rapidly breaks string beans in the pot.*)

Chris   Just because she isn't married doesn't mean she's been mourning Larry.

Mother (*with an undercurrent of observation*)   Why then isn't she?

Chris (*a little flustered*)   Well . . . it could've been any number of things.

Mother (*directly at him*)   Like what, for instance?

Chris (*embarrassed, but standing his ground*)   I don't know. Whatever it is. Can I get you an aspirin?

Mother *puts her hand to her head. She gets up and goes aimlessly toward the trees on rising.*

Mother   It's not like a headache.

Keller   You don't sleep, that's why. She's wearing out more bedroom slippers than shoes.

Mother   I had a terrible night. (*She stops moving.*) I never had a night like that.

Chris (*looking at* **Keller**)   What was it, Mom? Did you dream?

Mother   More, more than a dream.

Chris (*hesitantly*)   About Larry?

Mother   I was fast asleep, and – (*Raising her arm over the audience.*) Remember the way he used to fly low past the house when he was in training? When we used to see his face in the cockpit going by? That's the way I saw him. Only high up. Way, way up, where the clouds are. He was so real I could reach out and touch him. And suddenly he started to fall. And crying, crying to me . . . Mom, Mom! I could hear him like he was in the room. Mom! . . . it was his voice! If I could touch him I knew I could stop him, if I could only – (*Breaks off, allowing her outstretched hand to fall.*) I woke up and it was so funny – The wind . . . it was like the roaring of his engine. I came out here . . . I must've still been half asleep. I could hear that roaring like he was going by. The tree snapped right in front of me – and I like – came awake. (*She is looking at tree. She suddenly realizes something, turns with a reprimanding finger shaking slightly at* **Keller**.) See? We should never have planted that tree. I said so in the first place; it was too soon to plant a tree for him.

Chris (*alarmed*)   Too soon!

Mother (*angering*)   We rushed into it. Everybody was in such a hurry to bury him. I *said* not to plant it yet. (*To* **Keller**.) I *told* you to – !

Chris   Mother, Mother! (*She looks into his face.*) The wind blew it down. What significance has that got? What are you talking about? Mother, please . . . Don't go through it all again, will you? It's no good, it doesn't accomplish anything. I've been thinking, y'know? – maybe we ought to put our minds to forgetting him?

Mother   That's the third time you've said that this week.

Chris   Because it's not right; we never took up our lives again. We're like at a railroad station waiting for a train that never comes in.

Mother (*pressing top of her head*)   Get me an aspirin, heh?

Chris   Sure, and let's break out of this, heh, Mom? I thought the four of us might go out to dinner a couple of nights, maybe go dancing out at the shore.

Mother   Fine. (*To* **Keller**.) We can do it tonight.

Keller   Swell with me!

Chris   Sure, let's have some fun. (*To* **Mother**.) You'll start with this aspirin. (*He goes up and into house with new spirit. Her smile vanishes.*)

Mother (*with an accusing undertone*)   Why did he invite her here?

Keller   Why does that bother you?

Mother   She's been in New York three and a half years, why all of a sudden – ?

Keller   Well, maybe – maybe he just wanted to see her.

Mother   Nobody comes seven hundred miles 'just to see'.

Keller   What do you mean? He lived next door to the girl all his life, why shouldn't he want to see her again? (**Mother** *looks at him critically.*) Don't look at me like that, he didn't tell me any more than he told you.

Mother (*a warning and a question*)   He's not going to marry her.

Keller   How do you know he's even thinking of it?

Mother   It's got that about it.

Keller (*sharply watching her reaction*)   Well? So what?

Mother (*alarmed*)   What's going on here, Joe?

Keller   Now listen, kid –

Mother (*avoiding contact with him*)   She's not his girl, Joe; she knows she's not.

Keller   You can't read her mind.

Mother   Then why is she still single? New York is full of men, why isn't she married? (*Pause.*) Probably a hundred people told her she's foolish, but she's waited.

Keller   How do you know why she waited?

Mother   She knows what I know, that's why. She's faithful as a rock. In my worst moments, I think of her waiting, and I know again that I'm right.

Keller   Look, it's a nice day. What are we arguing for?

Mother (*warningly*)   Nobody in this house dast take her faith away, Joe. Strangers might. But not his father, not his brother.

Keller (*exasperated*)   What do you want me to do? What do you want?

Mother   I want you to act like he's coming back. Both of you. Don't think I haven't noticed you since Chris invited her. I won't stand for any nonsense.

Keller   But, Kate –

Mother   Because if he's not coming back, then I'll kill myself! Laugh. Laugh at me. (*She points to tree.*) But why did that happen the very night she came back? Laugh, but there are meanings in such things. She goes to sleep in his room and his memorial breaks in pieces. Look at it; look. (*She sits on bench.*) Joe –

Keller   Calm yourself.

Mother   Believe with me, Joe. I can't stand all alone.

Keller   Calm yourself.

Mother   Only last week a man turned up in Detroit, missing longer than Larry. You read it yourself.

Keller   All right, all right, calm yourself.

Mother   You above all have got to believe, you –

Keller (*rising*)   Why me above all?

Mother   Just don't stop believing.

Keller   What does that mean, me above all?

Bert *comes rushing on.*

Bert   Mr Keller! Say, Mr Keller . . . (*Pointing up driveway.*) Tommy just said it again!

Keller (*not remembering any of it*)   Said what? Who?

Bert   The dirty word.

Keller   Oh. Well –

Bert   Gee, aren't you going to arrest him? I warned him.

Mother (*with suddenness*)   Stop that, Bert. Go home. (**Bert** *backs up, as she advances.*) There's no jail here.

Keller (*as though to say, 'Oh-what-the-hell-let-him-believe-there-is'*)
Kate –

Mother (*turning on* **Keller** *furiously*)   There's no jail here! I want you to stop that jail business! (*He turns, shamed, but peeved.*)

Bert (*past her to* **Keller**)   He's right across the street.

Mother   Go home, Bert. (**Bert** *turns around and goes up driveway. She is shaken. Her speech is bitten off, extremely urgent.*) I want you to stop that, Joe. That whole jail business!

Keller (*alarmed, therefore angered*)   Look at you, look at you shaking.

Mother (*trying to control herself, moving about clasping her hands*) I can't help it.

Keller   What have I got to hide? What the hell is the matter with you, Kate?

Mother   I didn't say you had anything to hide, I'm just telling you to stop it! Now stop it! (*As* **Ann** *and* **Chris** *appear on porch.* **Ann** *is twenty-six, gentle but despite herself capable of holding fast to what she knows.* **Chris** *opens door for her.*)

Ann   Hya, Joe! (*She leads off a general laugh that is not self-conscious because they know one another too well.*)

Chris (*bringing* **Ann** *down, with an outstretched, chivalric arm*) Take a breath of that air, kid. You never get air like that in New York.

Mother (*genuinely overcome with it*)   Annie, where did you get that dress!

Ann   I couldn't resist. I'm taking it right off before I ruin it. (*Swings around.*) How's that for three weeks' salary?

Mother (*to* **Keller**)   Isn't she the most – ? (*To* **Ann**.) It's gorgeous, simply gor –

Chris (*to* **Mother**)   No kidding, now, isn't she the prettiest gal you ever saw?

Mother (*caught short by his obvious admiration, she finds herself reaching out for a glass of water and aspirin in his hand, and –*)   You gained a little weight, didn't you, darling? (*She gulps pill and drinks.*)

Ann   It comes and goes.

Keller   Look how nice her legs turned out!

Ann (*as she runs to fence*)   Boy, the poplars got thick, didn't they?

Keller *moves to settee and sits.*

Keller   Well, it's three years, Annie. We're gettin' old, kid.

Mother   How does Mom like New York? (**Ann** *keeps looking through trees.*)

Ann (*a little hurt*)   Why'd they take our hammock away?

Keller   Oh, no, it broke. Couple of years ago.

Mother   What broke? He had one of his light lunches and flopped into it.

Ann (*laughs and turns back toward* **Jim**'*s yard*)   Oh, excuse me!

Jim *has come to fence and is looking over it. He is smoking a cigar. As she cries out, he comes on around on stage.*

Jim   How do you do. (*To* **Chris**.) She looks very intelligent!

Chris   Ann, this is Jim – Doctor Bayliss.

Ann (*shaking* **Jim**'*s hand*)   Oh, sure, he writes a lot about you.

Jim   Don't you believe it. He likes everybody. In the battalion he was known as Mother McKeller.

Ann   I can believe it. You know – ? (*To* **Mother**.) It's so strange seeing him come out of that yard. (*To* **Chris**.) I guess I never grew up. It almost seems that Mom and Pop are in there now. And you and my brother doing algebra, and Larry trying to copy my homework. Gosh, those dear dead days beyond recall.

Jim   Well, I hope that doesn't mean you want me to move out?

Sue (*calling from offstage*)   Jim, come in here! Mr Hubbard is on the phone!

Jim   I told you I don't want –

Sue (*commandingly sweet*)   Please, dear! Please!

Jim (*resigned*)   All right, Susie. (*Trailing off.*) All right, all right . . . (*To* **Ann**.) I've only met you, Ann, but if I may offer you a piece of advice – When you marry, never – even in your mind – never count your husband's money.

Sue (*from offstage*)   Jim?

Jim   At once! (*Turns and goes off.*) At once. (*He exits.*)

Mother (**Ann** *is looking at her. She speaks meaningfully*)   I told her to take up the guitar. It'd be a common interest for them. (*They laugh.*) Well, he loves the guitar!

Ann, *as though to overcome* **Mother**, *becomes suddenly lively, crosses to* **Keller** *on settee, sits on his lap.*

Ann   Let's eat at the shore tonight! Raise some hell around here, like we used to before Larry went!

Mother (*emotionally*)   You think of him! You see? (*Triumphantly.*) She thinks of him!

Ann (*with an uncomprehending smile*)   What do you mean, Kate?

Mother   Nothing. Just that you – remember him, he's in your thoughts.

Ann   That's a funny thing to say; how could I help remembering him?

Mother (*it is drawing to a head the wrong way for her; she starts anew. She rises and comes to* **Ann**)   Did you hang up your things?

Ann   Yeah . . . (*To* **Chris**.) Say, you've sure gone in for clothes. I could hardly find room in the closet.

Mother   No, don't you remember? That's Larry's room.

Ann   You mean . . . they're Larry's?

Mother   Didn't you recognize them?

Ann (*slowly rising, a little embarrassed*)   Well, it never occurred to me that you'd – I mean the shoes are all shined.

Mother   Yes, dear. (*Slight pause.* **Ann** *can't stop staring at her.* **Mother** *breaks it by speaking with the relish of gossip, putting her arm around* **Ann** *and walking with her.*) For so long I've been aching for a nice conversation with you, Annie. Tell me something.

Ann   What?

Mother   I don't know. Something nice.

Chris (*wryly*)   She means do you go out much?

Mother   Oh, shut up.

Keller   And are any of them serious?

Mother (*laughing, sits in her chair*)   Why don't you both choke?

Keller   Annie, you can't go into a restaurant with that woman any more. In five minutes thirty-nine strange people are sitting at the table telling her their life story.

Mother   If I can't ask Annie a personal question –

Keller   Askin' is all right, but don't beat her over the head. You're beatin' her, you're beatin' her. (*They are laughing.*)

Ann *takes pan of beans off stool, puts them on floor under chair and sits.*

Ann (*to* **Mother**)   Don't let them bulldoze you. Ask me anything you like. What do you want to know, Kate? Come on, let's gossip.

Mother (*to* **Chris** *and* **Keller**)   She's the only one is got any sense. (*To* **Ann**.) Your mother – she's not getting a divorce, heh?

Ann   No, she's calmed down about it now. I think when he gets out they'll probably live together. In New York, of course.

Mother   That's fine. Because your father is still – I mean he's a decent man after all is said and done.

Ann   I don't care. She can take him back if she likes.

Mother   And you? You – (*Shakes her head negatively.*) go out much? (*Slight pause.*)

Ann (*delicately*)   You mean am I still waiting for him?

Mother   Well, no. I don't expect you to wait for him but –

Ann (*kindly*)   But that's what you mean, isn't it?

Mother   Well . . . yes.

Ann   Well, I'm not, Kate.

Mother (*faintly*)   You're not?

Ann   Isn't it ridiculous? You don't really imagine he's – ?

Mother   I know, dear, but don't say it's ridiculous, because the papers were full of it; I don't know about New York, but there was half a page about a man missing even longer than Larry, and he turned up from Burma.

Chris (*coming to* **Ann**)   He couldn't have wanted to come home very badly, Mom.

Mother   Don't be so smart.

Chris   You can have a helluva time in Burma.

Ann (*rises and swings around in back of* **Chris**)   So I've heard.

Chris   Mother, I'll bet you money that you're the only woman in the country who after three years is still –

Mother   You're sure?

Chris   Yes, I am.

Mother   Well, if you're sure then you're sure. (*She turns her head away an instant.*) They don't say it on the radio but I'm sure that in the dark at night they're still waiting for their sons.

Chris   Mother, you're absolutely –

Mother (*waving him off*)   Don't be so damned smart! Now stop it! (*Slight pause.*) There are just a few things you *don't* know. All of you. And I'll tell you one of them, Annie. Deep, deep in your heart you've always been waiting for him.

Ann (*resolutely*)   No, Kate.

Mother (*with increasing demand*)   But deep in your heart, Annie!

Chris   She ought to know, shouldn't she?

Mother   Don't let them tell you what to think. Listen to your heart. Only your heart.

Ann   Why does your heart tell you he's alive?

Mother   Because he has to be.

Ann   But why, Kate?

Mother (*going to her*)   Because certain things have to be, and certain things can never be. Like the sun has to rise, it has to be. That's why there's God. Otherwise anything could happen. But there's God, so certain things can never happen. I would know, Annie – just like I knew the day he – (*Indicates* **Chris**.) went into that terrible battle. Did he write me? Was it in the papers? No, but that morning I couldn't raise my head off the pillow. Ask Joe. Suddenly, I knew. I knew! And he was nearly killed that day. Ann, you *know* I'm right!

Ann *stands there in silence, then turns trembling, going upstage.*

Ann   No, Kate.

Mother   I have to have some tea.

Frank *appears, carrying ladder.*

Frank   Annie! (*Coming down.*) How are you, gee whiz!

Ann (*taking his hand*)   Why, Frank, you're losing your hair.

Keller   He's got responsibility.

Frank   Gee whiz!

Keller   Without Frank the stars wouldn't know when to come out.

Frank (*laughs; to* **Ann**)   You look more womanly. You've matured. You –

Keller   Take it easy, Frank, you're a married man.

Ann (*as they laugh*)   You still haberdashering?

Frank   Why not? Maybe I too can get to be president. How's your brother? Got his degree, I hear.

Ann   Oh, George has his own office now!

Frank   Don't say! (*Funereally.*) And your dad? Is he – ?

Ann (*abruptly*)   Fine. I'll be in to see Lydia.

Frank (*sympathetically*)   How about it, does Dad expect a parole soon?

Ann (*with growing ill-ease*)   I really don't know, I –

Frank (*staunchly defending her father for her sake*)   I mean because I feel, y'know, that if an intelligent man like your father is put in prison, there ought to be a law that says either you execute him, or let him go after a year.

Chris (*interrupting*)   Want a hand with that ladder, Frank?

Frank (*taking cue*)   That's all right, I'll – (*Picks up ladder.*) I'll finish the horoscope tonight, Kate. (*Embarrassed.*) See you later, Ann, you look wonderful. (*He exits. They look at* **Ann**.)

Ann (*to* **Chris**, *as she sits slowly on stool*)   Haven't they stopped talking abut Dad?

Chris (*comes down and sits on arm of chair*)   Nobody talks about him any more.

Keller (*rises and comes to her*)   Gone and forgotten, kid.

Ann   Tell me. Because I don't want to meet anybody on the block if they're going to –

Chris   I don't want you to worry about it.

Ann (*to* **Keller**)   Do they still remember the case, Joe? Do they talk about you?

Keller   The only one still talks about it is my wife.

Mother   That's because you keep on playing policeman with the kids. All their parents hear out of you is jail, jail, jail.

Keller   Actually what happened was that when I got home from the penitentiary the kids got very interested in me. You know kids. I was – (*Laughs.*) like the expert on the jail situation. And as time passed they got it confused and . . . I ended up a detective. (*Laughs.*)

Mother   Except that *they* didn't get it confused. (*To* **Ann**.) He hands out police badges from the Post Toasties boxes. (*They laugh.*)

Ann *rises and comes to* **Keller**, *putting her arm around his shoulder.*

Ann (*wondrously at them, happy*)   Gosh, it's wonderful to hear you laughing about it.

Chris   Why, what'd you expect?

Ann   The last thing I remember on this block was one word – 'Murderers!' Remember that, Kate? – Mrs Hammond standing in front of our house and yelling that word? She's still around, I suppose?

Mother   They're all still around.

Keller   Don't listen to her. Every Saturday night the whole gang is playin' poker in this arbor. All the ones who yelled murderer takin' my money now.

Mother   Don't, Joe; she's a sensitive girl, don't fool her. (*To* **Ann**.) They still remember about Dad. It's different with him. (*Indicates* **Joe**.) He was exonerated, your father's still there. That's why I wasn't so enthusiastic about your coming. Honestly, I know how sensitive you are, and I told Chris, I said –

Keller   Listen, you do like I did and you'll be all right. The day I come home, I got out of my car – but not in front of the house . . . on the corner. You should've been here, Annie, and you too, Chris; you'd-a seen something. Everybody knew I was getting out that day; the porches were loaded. Picture it now; none of them believed I was innocent. The story was, I pulled a fast one getting myself exonerated. So I get out of my car, and I walk down the street. But very slow. And with a smile. The beast! I was the beast; the guy who sold cracked cylinder heads to the Army Air Force; the guy who made twenty-one P-40s crash in Australia. Kid, walkin' down the street that day I was guilty as hell. Except I wasn't, and there was a court paper in my pocket to prove I wasn't, and I walked . . . past . . . the porches. Result? Fourteen months later I had one of the best shops in the state again, a respected man again; bigger than ever.

Chris (*with admiration*)   Joe McGuts.

Keller (*now with great force*)   That's the only way you lick 'em is guts! (*To* **Ann**.) The worst thing you did was to move away from here. You made it tough for your father when he gets out. That's why I tell you, I like to see him move back right on this block.

Mother (*pained*)   How could they move back?

Keller   It ain't gonna end *till* they move back! (*To* **Ann**.) Till people play cards with him again, and talk with him, and smile with him – you play cards with a man you know he can't be a murderer. And the next time you write him I like you to tell him just what I said. (**Ann** *simply stares at him.*) You hear me?

Ann (*surprised*)   Don't you hold anything against him?

Keller   Annie, I never believed in crucifying people.

Ann (*mystified*)   But he was your partner, he dragged you through the mud.

Keller   Well, he ain't my sweetheart, but you gotta forgive, don't you?

Ann   You, either, Kate? Don't you feel any – ?

Keller (*to* **Ann**)   The next time you write Dad –

Ann   I don't write him.

Keller (*struck*)   Well, every now and then you –

Ann (*a little shamed, but determined*)   No, I've *never* written to him. Neither has my brother. (*To* **Chris**.) Say, do you feel this way, too?

Chris   He murdered twenty-one pilots.

Keller   What the hell kind a talk is that?

Mother   That's not a thing to say about a man.

Ann   What else can you say? When they took him away I followed him, went to him every visiting day. I was crying all the time. Until the news came about Larry. Then I realized. It's wrong to pity a man like that. Father or no father, there's only one way to look at him. He knowingly shipped out parts that would crash an airplane. And how do you know Larry wasn't one of them?

Mother   I was waiting for that. (*Going to her.*) As long as you're here, Annie, I want to ask you never to say that again.

Ann   You surprise me. I thought you'd be mad at him.

Mother   What your father did had nothing to do with Larry. Nothing.

Ann   But we can't know that.

Mother (*striving for control*)   As long as you're here!

Ann (*perplexed*)   But, Kate –

Mother   Put that out of your head!

Keller   Because –

Mother (*quickly to* **Keller**)   That's all, that's enough. (*Places her hand on her head.*) Come inside now, and have some tea with me. (*She turns and goes up steps.*)

Keller (*to* **Ann**)   The one thing you –

Mother (*sharply*)   He's not dead, so there's no argument!
Now come!

Keller (*angrily*)   In a minute! (**Mother** *turns and goes into house.*)
Now look, Annie –

Chris   All right, Dad, forget it.

Keller   No, she dasn't feel that way. Annie –

Chris   I'm sick of the whole subject, now cut it out.

Keller   You want her to go on like this? (*To* **Ann**.) Those
cylinder heads went into P-40s only. What's the matter with
you? You know Larry never flew a P-40.

Chris   So who flew those P-40s, pigs?

Keller   The man was a fool, but don't make a murderer out
of him. You got no sense? Look what it does to her! (*To* **Ann**.)
Listen, you gotta appreciate what was doin' in that shop in the
war. The both of you! It was a madhouse. Every half hour the
Major callin' for cylinder heads, they were whippin' us with
the telephone. The trucks were hauling them away hot, damn
near. I mean just try to see it human, see it human. All of a
sudden a batch comes out with a crack. That happens, that's
the business. A fine, hairline crack. All right, so – so he's a little
man, your father, always scared of loud voices. What'll the
Major say? – Half a day's production shot . . . What'll I say?
You know what I mean? Human. (*He pauses.*) So he takes out
his tools and he – covers over the cracks. All right – that's bad,
it's wrong, but that's what a little man does. If I could have
gone in that day I'd a told him – junk 'em, Steve, we can
afford it. But alone he was afraid. But I know he meant no
harm. He believed they'd hold up a hundred per cent. That's a
mistake, but it ain't murder. You mustn't feel that way about
him. You understand me? It ain't right.

Ann (*she regards him a moment*)   Joe, let's forget it.

Keller   Annie, the day the news came about Larry he was in
the next cell to mine – Dad. And he cried, Annie – he cried
half the night.

Ann (*touched*)   He shoulda cried all night. (*Slight pause.*)

Keller (*almost angered*)   Annie, I do not understand why you – !

Chris (*breaking in – with nervous urgency*)   Are you going to stop it?

Ann   Don't yell at him. He just wants everybody happy.

Keller (*clasps her around waist, smiling*)   That's my sentiments. Can you stand steak?

Chris   And champagne!

Keller   Now you're operatin'! I'll call Swanson's for a table! Big time tonight, Annie.

Ann   Can't scare me.

Keller (*to* **Chris**, *pointing at* **Ann**)   I like that girl. Wrap her up. (*They laugh. Goes up porch.*) You got nice legs, Annie! . . . I want to see everybody drunk tonight. (*Pointing to* **Chris**.) Look at him, he's blushin'! (*He exits, laughing, into house.*)

Chris (*calling after him*)   Drink your tea, Casanova. (*He turns to* **Ann**.) Isn't he a great guy?

Ann   You're the only one I know who loves his parents.

Chris   I know. It went out of style, didn't it?

Ann (*with a sudden touch of sadness*)   It's all right. It's a good thing. (*She looks about.*) You know? It's lovely here. The air is sweet.

Chris (*hopefully*)   You're not sorry you came?

Ann   Not sorry, no. But I'm – not going to stay.

Chris   Why?

Ann   In the first place, your mother as much as told me to go.

Chris   Well –

Ann   You saw that – and then you – you've been kind of –

Chris   What?

Ann   Well . . . kind of embarrassed ever since I got here.

Chris   The trouble is I planned on kind of sneaking up on you over a period of a week or so. But they take it for granted that we're all set.

Ann   I knew they would. Your mother anyway.

Chris   How did you know?

Ann   From *her* point of view, why else would I come?

Chris   Well . . . would you want to? (**Ann** *still studies him.*) I guess you know this is why I asked you to come.

Ann   I guess this is why I came.

Chris   Ann, I love you. I love you a great deal. (*Finally.*) I love you. (*Pause. She waits.*) I have no imagination . . . that's all I know to tell you. (**Ann** *is waiting, ready.*) I'm embarrassing you. I didn't want to tell it to you here. I wanted some place we'd never been; a place where we'd be brand new to each other . . . You feel it's wrong here, don't you? This yard, this chair? I want you to be ready for me. I don't want to win you away from anything.

Ann (*putting her arms around him*)   Oh, Chris, I've been ready a long, long time!

Chris   Then he's gone forever. You're sure.

Ann   I almost got married two years ago.

Chris   Why didn't you?

Ann   You started to write to me – (*Slight pause.*)

Chris   You felt something that far back?

Ann   Every day since!

Chris   Ann, why didn't you let me know?

Ann   I was waiting for you, Chris. Till then you never wrote. And when you did, what did you say? You sure can be ambiguous, you know.

Chris (*looks toward house, then at her, trembling*)   Give me a kiss, Ann. Give me a – (*They kiss.*) God, I kissed you, Annie, I kissed Annie. How long, how long I've been waiting to kiss you!

Ann   I'll never forgive you. Why did you wait all these years? All I've done is sit and wonder if I was crazy for thinking of you.

Chris   Annie, we're going to live now! I'm going to make you so happy. (*He kisses her, but without their bodies touching.*)

Ann (*a little embarrassed*)   Not like that you're not.

Chris   I kissed you . . .

Ann   Like Larry's brother. Do it like you, Chris. (*He breaks away from her abruptly.*) What is it, Chris?

Chris   Let's drive some place . . . I want to be alone with you.

Ann   No . . . what is it, Chris, your mother?

Chris   No – nothing like that.

Ann   Then what's wrong? Even in your letters, there was something ashamed.

Chris   Yes. I suppose I have been. But it's going from me.

Ann   You've got to tell me –

Chris   I don't know how to start. (*He takes her hand.*)

Ann   It wouldn't work this way. (*Slight pause.*)

Chris (*speaks quietly, factually at first*)   It's all mixed up with so many other things . . . You remember, overseas, I was in command of a company?

Ann   Yeah, sure.

Chris   Well, I lost them.

Ann   How many?

Chris   Just about all.

Ann   Oh, gee!

Chris   It takes a little time to toss that off. Because they
weren't just men. For instance, one time it'd been raining
several days and this kid came to me, and gave me his last pair
of dry socks. Put them in my pocket. That's only a little thing –
but . . . that's the kind of guys I had. They didn't die; they
killed themselves for each other. I mean that exactly; a little
more selfish and they'd've been here today. And I got an idea –
watching them go down. Everything was being destroyed, see,
but it seemed to me that one new thing was made. A kind of –
responsibility. Man for man. You understand me? – To show
that, to bring that onto the earth again like some kind of a
monument and everyone would feel it standing there, behind
him, and it would make a difference to him. (*Pause.*) And then
I came home and it was incredible. I – there was no meaning in
it here; the whole thing to them was a kind of a – bus accident.
I went to work with Dad, and that rat-race again. I felt – what
you said – ashamed somehow. Because nobody was changed at
all. It seemed to make suckers out of a lot of guys. I felt wrong
to be alive, to open the bank-book, to drive the new car, to see
the new refrigerator. I mean you can take those things out of
a war, but when you drive that car you've got to know that it
came out of the love a man can have for a man, you've got to
be a little better because of that. Otherwise what you have is
really loot, and there's blood on it. I didn't want to take any
of it. And I guess that included you.

Ann   And you still feel that way?

Chris   I want you now, Annie.

Ann   Because you mustn't feel that way any more. Because you
have a right to whatever you have. Everything, Chris, understand
that? To me, too . . . And the money, there's nothing wrong in
your money. Your father put hundreds of planes in the air, you
should be proud. A man should be paid for that . . .

Chris   Oh Annie, Annie . . . I'm going to make a fortune for
you!

Keller (*offstage*)   Hello . . . Yes. Sure.

Ann (*laughing softly*)   What'll I do with a fortune?

They kiss. **Keller** *enters from house.*

Keller (*thumbing toward house*)   Hey, Ann, your brother – (*They step apart shyly.* **Keller** *comes down, and wryly:*) What is this, Labor Day?

Chris (*waving him away, knowing the kidding will be endless*)   All right, all right.

Ann   You shouldn't burst out like that.

Keller   Well, nobody told me it was Labor Day. (*Looks around.*) Where's the hot dogs?

Chris (*loving it*)   All right. You said it once.

Keller   Well, as long as I know it's Labor Day from now on, I'll wear a bell around my neck.

Ann (*affectionately*)   He's so subtle!

Chris   George Bernard Shaw as an elephant.

Keller   George! – hey, you kissed it out of my head – your brother's on the phone.

Ann (*surprised*)   My brother?

Keller   Yeah, George. Long distance.

Ann   What's the matter, is anything wrong?

Keller   I don't know, Kate's talking to him. Hurry up, she'll cost him five dollars.

Ann (*takes a step upstage, then comes down toward* **Chris**)   I wonder if we ought to tell your mother yet? I mean I'm not very good in an argument.

Chris   We'll wait till tonight. After dinner. Now don't get tense, just leave it to me.

Keller   What're you telling her?

Chris   Go ahead, Ann. (*With misgivings,* **Ann** *goes up and into house.*) We're getting married, Dad. (**Keller** *nods indecisively.*) Well, don't you say anything?

Keller (*distracted*)   I'm glad, Chris, I'm just – George is calling from Columbus.

Chris   Columbus!

Keller   Did Annie tell you he was going to see his father today?

Chris   No, I don't think she knew anything about it.

Keller (*asking uncomfortably*)   Chris! You – you think you know her pretty good?

Chris (*hurt and apprehensive*)   What kind of a question?

Keller   I'm just wondering. All these years George don't go to see his father. Suddenly he goes . . . and she comes here.

Chris   Well, what about it?

Keller   It's crazy, but it comes to my mind. She don't hold nothin' against me, does she?

Chris (*angry*)   I don't know what you're talking about.

Keller (*a little more combatively*)   I'm just talkin'. To his last day in court the man blamed it all on me; and this is his daughter. I mean if she was sent here to find out something?

Chris (*angered*)   Why? What is there to find out?

Ann (*on phone, offstage*)   Why are you so excited, George? What happened there?

Keller   I mean if they want to open up the case again, for the nuisance value, to hurt us?

Chris   Dad . . . how could you think that of her?

Ann (*simultaneously; still on phone*)   But what did he say to you, for God's sake?

Keller   It couldn't be, heh. You know.

Chris   Dad, you amaze me . . .

Keller (*breaking in*) All right, forget it, forget it. (*With great force, moving about.*) I want a clean start for you, Chris. I want a new sign over the plant – Christopher Keller, Incorporated.

Chris (*a little uneasily*) J. O. Keller is good enough.

Keller We'll talk about it. I'm going to build you a house, stone, with a driveway from the road. I want you to spread out, Chris, I want you to use what I made for you. (*He is close to him now.*) I mean, with joy, Chris, without shame . . . with joy.

Chris (*touched*) I will, Dad.

Keller (*with deep emotion*) Say it to me.

Chris Why?

Keller Because sometimes I think you're . . . ashamed of the money.

Chris No, don't feel that.

Keller Because it's good money, there's nothing wrong with that money.

Chris (*a little frightened*) Dad, you don't have to tell me this.

Keller (*with overriding affection and self-confidence now. He grips* **Chris** *by the back of the neck, and with laughter between his determined jaws*) Look, Chris, I'll go to work on Mother for you. We'll get her so drunk tonight we'll all get married! (*Steps away, with a wide gesture of his arm.*) There's gonna be a wedding, kid, like there never was seen! Champagne, tuxedos – !

He breaks off as **Ann**'s *voice comes out loud from the house where she is still talking on phone.*

Ann Simply because when you get excited you don't control yourself . . . (**Mother** *comes out of house.*) Well, what did he tell you for God's sake? (*Pause.*) All right, come then. (*Pause.*) Yes, they'll all be here. Nobody's running away from you. And try to get hold of yourself, will you? (*Pause.*) All right, all right. Good-by. (*There is a brief pause as* **Ann** *hangs up receiver, then comes out of kitchen.*)

Chris   Something happen?

Keller   He's coming here?

Ann   On the seven o'clock. He's in Columbus. (*To* **Mother**.)
I told him it would be all right.

Keller   Sure, fine! Your father took sick?

Ann (*mystified*)   No, George didn't say he was sick. I – (*Shaking it off.*) I don't know, I suppose it's something stupid, you know my brother – (*She comes to* **Chris**.) Let's go for a drive, or something . . .

Chris   Sure. Give me the keys, Dad.

Mother   Drive through the park. It's beautiful now.

Chris   Come on, Ann. (*To them.*) Be back right away.

Ann (*as she and* **Chris** *exit up driveway*)   See you.

Mother *comes down toward* **Keller**, *her eyes fixed on him.*

Keller   Take your time. (*To* **Mother**.) What does George want?

Mother   He's been in Columbus since this morning with Steve. He's gotta see Annie right away, he says.

Keller   What for?

Mother   I don't know. (*She speaks with warning.*) He's a lawyer now, Joe. George is a lawyer. All these years he never even sent a postcard to Steve. Since he got back from the war, not a postcard.

Keller   So what?

Mother (*her tension breaking out*)   Suddenly he takes an airplane from New York to see him. An airplane!

Keller   Well? So?

Mother (*trembling*)   Why?

Keller   I don't read minds. Do you?

Mother   Why, Joe? What has Steve suddenly got to tell him that he takes an airplane to see him?

Keller   What do I care what Steve's got to tell him?

Mother   You're sure, Joe?

Keller (*frightened, but angry*)   Yes, I'm sure.

Mother (*sits stiffly in a chair*)   Be smart now, Joe. The boy is coming. Be smart.

Keller (*desperately*)   Once and for all, did you hear what I said? I said I'm sure!

Mother (*nods weakly*)   All right, Joe. (*He straightens up.*) Just . . . be smart.

Keller, *in hopeless fury, looks at her, turns around, goes up to porch and into house, slamming screen door violently behind him.* **Mother** *sits in chair downstage, stiffly, staring, seeing.*

Curtain.

Act Two

As twilight falls, that evening.

On the rise, **Chris** *is discovered sawing the broken-off tree, leaving stump standing alone. He is dressed in good pants, white shoes, but without a shirt. He disappears with tree up the alley when* **Mother** *appears on porch. She comes down and stands watching him. She has on a dressing gown, carries a tray of grape-juice drink in a pitcher, and glasses with sprigs of mint in them.*

Mother (*calling up alley*) Did you have to put on good pants to do that? (*She comes downstage and puts tray on table in the arbor. Then looks around uneasily, then feels pitcher for coolness.* **Chris** *enters from alley brushing off his hands.*) You notice there's more light with that thing gone?

Chris Why aren't you dressing?

Mother It's suffocating upstairs. I made a grape drink for Georgie. He always liked grape. Come and have some.

Chris (*impatiently*) Well, come on, get dressed. And what's Dad sleeping so much for? (*He goes to table and pours a glass of juice.*)

Mother He's worried. When he's worried he sleeps. (*Pauses. Looks into his eyes.*) We're dumb, Chris. Dad and I are stupid people. We don't know anything. You've got to protect us.

Chris You're silly; what's there to be afraid of?

Mother To his last day in court Steve never gave up the idea that Dad made him do it. If they're going to open the case again I won't live through it.

Chris George is just a damn fool, Mother. How can you take him seriously?

Mother That family hates us. Maybe even Annie –

Chris Oh, now, Mother . . .

Mother   You think just because you like everybody, they like you!

Chris   All right, stop working yourself up. Just leave everything to me.

Mother   When George goes home tell her to go with him.

Chris (*noncommittally*)   Don't worry about Annie.

Mother   Steve is her father, too.

Chris   Are you going to cut it out? Now, come.

Mother (*going upstage with him*)   You don't realize how people can hate, Chris, they can hate so much they'll tear the world to pieces.

Ann, *dressed up, appears on porch.*

Chris   Look! She's dressed already. (*As he and* **Mother** *mount porch.*) I've just got to put on a shirt.

Ann (*in a preoccupied way*)   Are you feeling well, Kate?

Mother   What's the difference, dear. There are certain people, y'know, the sicker they get the longer they live. (*She goes into house.*)

Chris   You look nice.

Ann   We're going to tell her tonight.

Chris   Absolutely, don't worry about it.

Ann   I wish we could tell her now. I can't stand scheming. My stomach gets hard.

Chris   It's not scheming, we'll just get her in a better mood.

Mother (*offstage, in the house*)   Joe, are you going to sleep all day!

Ann (*laughing*)   The only one who's relaxed is your father. He's fast asleep.

Chris   I'm relaxed.

Ann   Are you?

Chris   Look. (*He holds out his hand and makes it shake.*) Let me know when George gets here.

He goes into the house. **Ann** *moves aimlessly, and then is drawn toward tree stump. She goes to it, hesitantly touches broken top in the hush of her thoughts. Offstage* **Lydia** *calls, 'Johnny! Come get your supper!'* **Sue** *enters, and halts, seeing* **Ann**.

Sue   Is my husband – ?

Ann (*turns, startled*)   Oh!

Sue   I'm terribly sorry.

Ann   It's all right, I – I'm a little silly about the dark.

Sue (*looks about*)   It is getting dark.

Ann   Are you looking for your husband?

Sue   As usual. (*Laughs tiredly.*) He spends so much time here, they'll be charging him rent.

Ann   Nobody was dressed so he drove over to the depot to pick up my brother.

Sue   Oh, your brother's in?

Ann   Yeah, they ought to be here any minute now. Will you have a cold drink?

Sue   I will, thanks. (**Ann** *goes to table and pours.*) My husband. Too hot to drive me to beach. Men are like little boys; for the neighbors they'll always cut the grass.

Ann   People like to do things for the Kellers. Been that way since I can remember.

Sue   It's amazing. I guess your brother's coming to give you away, heh?

Ann (*giving her drink*)   I don't know. I suppose.

Sue   You must be all nerved up.

Ann   It's always a problem getting yourself married, isn't it?

Sue   That depends on your shape, of course. I don't see why you should have had a problem.

Ann   I've had chances –

Sue   I'll bet. It's romantic . . . it's very unusual to me, marrying the brother of your sweetheart.

Ann   I don't know. I think it's mostly that whenever I need somebody to tell me the truth I've always thought of Chris. When he tells you something you know it's so. He relaxes me.

Sue   And he's got money. That's important, you know.

Ann   It wouldn't matter to me.

Sue   You'd be surprised. It makes all the difference. I married an intern. On my salary. And that was bad, because as soon as a woman supports a man he owes her something. You can never owe somebody without resenting them. (**Ann** *laughs*.) That's true, you know.

Ann   Underneath, I think the doctor is very devoted.

Sue   Oh, certainly. But it's bad when a man always sees the bars in front of him. Jim thinks he's in jail all the time.

Ann   Oh . . .

Sue   That's why I've been intending to ask you a small favor, Ann. It's something very important to me.

Ann   Certainly, if I can do it.

Sue   You can. When you take up housekeeping, try to find a place away from here.

Ann   Are you fooling?

Sue   I'm very serious. My husband is unhappy with Chris around.

Ann   How is that?

Sue   Jim's a successful doctor. But he's got an idea he'd like to do medical research. Discover things. You see?

Ann   Well, isn't that good?

Sue   Research pays twenty-five dollars a week minus laundering the hair shirt. You've got to give up your life to go into it.

Ann   How does Chris –

Sue (*with growing feeling*)   Chris makes people want to be better than it's possible to be. He does that to people.

Ann   Is that bad?

Sue   My husband has a family, dear. Every time he has a session with Chris he feels as though he's compromising by not giving up everything for research. As though Chris or anybody else isn't compromising. It happens with Jim every couple of years. He meets a man and makes a statue out of him.

Ann   Maybe he's right. I don't mean that Chris is a statue, but –

Sue   Now darling, you know he's not right.

Ann   I don't agree with you. Chris –

Sue   Let's face it, dear. Chris is working with his father, isn't he? He's taking money out of that business every week in the year.

Ann   What of it?

Sue   You ask me what of it?

Ann   I certainly do. (*She seems about to burst out.*) You oughtn't cast aspersions like that, I'm surprised at you.

Sue   You're surprised at me!

Ann   He'd never take five cents out of that plant if there was anything wrong with it.

Sue   You know that.

Ann   I know it. I resent everything you've said.

Sue (*moving toward her*)   You know what I resent, dear?

Ann   Please, I don't want to argue.

Sue   I resent living next door to the Holy Family. It makes me look like a bum, you understand?

Ann   I can't do anything about that.

Sue   Who is he to ruin a man's life? Everybody knows Joe pulled a fast one to get out of jail.

Ann   That's not true!

Sue   Then why don't you go out and talk to people? Go on, talk to them. There's not a person on the block who doesn't know the truth.

Ann   That's a lie. People come here all the time for cards and –

Sue   So what? They give him credit for being smart. I do, too, I've got nothing against Joe. But if Chris wants people to put on the hair shirt let him take off his broadcloth. He's driving my husband crazy with that phony idealism of his, and I'm at the end of my rope on it! (**Chris** *enters on porch, wearing shirt and tie now. She turns quickly, hearing. With a smile.*) Hello, darling. How's Mother?

Chris   I thought George came.

Sue   No, it was just us.

Chris (*coming down to them*)   Susie, do me a favor, heh? Go up to Mother and see if you can calm her. She's all worked up.

Sue   She still doesn't know about you two?

Chris (*laughs a little*)   Well, she senses it, I guess. You know my mother.

Sue (*going up to porch*)   Oh, yeah, she's psychic.

Chris   Maybe there's something in the medicine chest.

Sue   I'll give her one of everything. (*On porch.*) Don't worry about Kate; couple of drinks, dance her around a little . . . She'll love Ann. (*To* **Ann**.) Because you're the female version of him. (**Chris** *laughs.*) Don't be alarmed, I said version. (*She goes into house.*)

Chris   Interesting woman, isn't she?

Ann   Yeah, she's very interesting.

Chris   She's a great nurse, you know, she –

Ann (*in tension, but trying to control it*)   Are you still doing that?

Chris (*sensing something wrong, but still smiling*)   Doing what?

Ann   As soon as you get to know somebody you find a distinction for them. How do you know she's a great nurse?

Chris   What's the matter, Ann?

Ann   The woman hates you. She despises you!

Chris   Hey . . . What's hit you?

Ann   Gee, Chris –

Chris   What happened here?

Ann   You never – Why didn't you tell me?

Chris   Tell you what?

Ann   She says they think Joe is guilty.

Chris   What difference does it make what they think?

Ann   I don't care what they think, I just don't understand why you took the trouble to deny it. You said it was all forgotten.

Chris   I didn't want you to feel there was anything wrong in you coming here, that's all. I know a lot of people think my father was guilty, and I assumed there might be some question in your mind.

Ann   But I never once said I suspected him.

Chris   Nobody says it.

Ann   Chris, I know how much you love him, but it could never –

Chris   Do you think I could forgive him if he'd done that thing?

Ann   I'm not here out of a blue sky, Chris. I turned my back on my father, if there's anything wrong here now –

Chris   I know that, Ann.

Ann   George is coming from Dad, and I don't think it's with a blessing.

Chris   He's welcome here. You've got nothing to fear from George.

Ann   Tell me that . . . Just tell me that.

Chris   The man is innocent, Ann. Remember he was falsely accused once and it put him through hell. How would you behave if you were faced with the same thing again? Annie, believe me, there's nothing wrong for you here, believe me, kid.

Ann   All right, Chris, all right. (*They embrace as* **Keller** *appears quietly on porch.* **Ann** *simply studies him.*)

Keller   Every time I come out here it looks like Playland! (*They break and laugh in embarrassment.*)

Chris   I thought you were going to shave?

Keller (*sitting on bench*)   In a minute. I just woke up, I can't see nothin'.

Ann   You look shaved.

Keller   Oh, no. (*Massages his jaw.*) Gotta be extra special tonight. Big night, Annie. So how's it feel to be a married woman?

Ann (*laughs*)   I don't know, yet.

Keller (*to* **Chris**)   What's the matter, you slippin'? (*He takes a little box of apples from under the bench as they talk.*)

Chris   The great roué!

Keller   What is that, roué?

Chris   It's French.

Keller   Don't talk dirty. (*They laugh.*)

Chris (*to* **Ann**)   You ever meet a bigger ignoramus?

Keller   Well, somebody's got to make a living.

Ann (*as they laugh*)   That's telling him.

Keller   I don't know, everybody's gettin' so goddam educated in this country there'll be nobody to take away the garbage. (*They laugh.*) It's gettin' so the only dumb ones left are the bosses.

Ann   You're not so dumb, Joe.

Keller   I know, but you go into our plant, for instance. I got so many lieutenants, majors and colonels that I'm ashamed to ask somebody to sweep the floor. I gotta be careful I'll insult somebody. No kiddin'. It's a tragedy: you stand on the street today and spit, you're gonna hit a college man.

Chris   Well, don't spit.

Keller (*breaks apple in half, passing it to* **Ann** *and* **Chris**)   I mean to say, it's comin' to a pass. (*He takes a breath.*) I been thinkin', Annie . . . your brother, George. I been thinkin' about your brother George. When he comes I like you to *brooch* something to him.

Chris   Broach.

Keller   What's the matter with brooch?

Chris (*smiling*)   It's not English.

Keller   When I went to night school it was brooch.

Ann (*laughing*)   Well, in day school it's broach.

Keller   Don't surround me, will you? Seriously, Ann . . . You say he's not well. George, I been thinkin', why should he knock himself out in New York with that cut-throat competition, when I got so many friends here; I'm very friendly with some big lawyers in town. I could set George up here.

Ann   That's awfully nice of you, Joe.

Keller   No, kid, it ain't nice of me. I want you to understand me. I'm thinking of Chris. (*Slight panic.*) See . . . this is what I mean. You get older, you want to feel that you – accomplished something. My only accomplishment is my son. I ain't brainy. That's all I accomplished. Now, a year, eighteen months, your father'll be a free man. Who is he going to come to, Annie? His baby. You. He'll come, old, mad, into your house.

Ann   That can't matter any more, Joe.

Keller   I don't want that to come between us. (*Gestures between* **Chris** *and himself.*)

Ann   I can only tell you that that could never happen.

Keller   You're in love now, Annie, but believe me, I'm older than you and I know – a daughter is a daughter, and a father is a father. And it could happen. (*He pauses.*) I like you and George to go to him in prison and tell him . . . 'Dad, Joe wants to bring you into the business when you get out.'

Ann (*surprised, even shocked*)   You'd have him as a partner?

Keller   No, no partner. A good job. (*Pause. He sees she is shocked, a little mystified. He gets up, speaks more nervously.*) I want him to know, Annie . . . while he's sitting there I want him to know that when he gets out he's got a place waitin' for him. It'll take his bitterness away. To know you got a place . . . it sweetens you.

Ann   Joe, you owe him nothing.

Keller   I owe him a good kick in the teeth, but he's your father.

Chris   Then kick him in the teeth! I don't want him in the plant, so that's that! You understand? And besides, don't talk about him like that. People misunderstand you!

Keller   And I don't understand why she has to crucify the man.

Chris   Well, it's her father, if she feels –

Keller   No, no.

Chris (*almost angrily*)   What's it to you? Why – ?

Keller (*commanding outburst in high nervousness*)   A father is a father! (*As though the outburst had revealed him, he looks about, wanting to retract it. His hand goes to his cheek.*) I better – I better shave. (*He turns and a smile is on his face. To* **Ann**.) I didn't mean to yell at you, Annie.

Ann   Let's forget the whole thing, Joe.

Keller   Right. (*To* **Chris**.) She's likeable.

Chris (*a little peeved at the man's stupidity*)   Shave, will you?

Keller   Right again.

As he turns to porch **Lydia** *comes hurrying from her house.*

Lydia   I forgot all about it. (*Seeing* **Chris** *and* **Ann**.) Hya. (*To* **Joe**.) I promised to fix Kate's hair for tonight. Did she comb it yet?

Keller   Always a smile, hey, Lydia?

Lydia   Sure, why not?

Keller (*going up on porch*)   Come on up and comb my Katie's hair. (**Lydia** *goes up on porch.*) She's got a big night, make her beautiful.

Lydia   I will.

Keller (*holds door open for her and she goes into kitchen. To* **Chris** *and* **Ann**)   Hey, that could be a song. (*He sings softly.*)

'Come on up and comb my Katie's hair . . .
Oh, come on up, 'cause she's my lady fair – '

(*To* **Ann**.) How's that for one year of night school? (*He continues singing as he goes into kitchen.*)

'Oh, come on up, come on up, and comb my lady's hair – '

Jim Bayliss *rounds corner of driveway, walking rapidly.* **Jim** *crosses to* **Chris**, *motions him and pulls him down excitedly.* **Keller** *stands just inside kitchen door, watching them.*

Chris   What's the matter? Where is he?

Jim   Where's your mother?

Chris   Upstairs, dressing.

Ann (*crossing to them rapidly*)   What happened to George?

Jim   I asked him to wait in the car. Listen to me now. Can you take some advice? (*They wait.*) Don't bring him in here.

Ann   Why?

Jim   Kate is in bad shape, you can't explode this in front of her.

Ann   Explode what?

Jim   You know why he's here, don't try to kid it away. There's blood in his eye; drive him somewhere and talk to him alone.

Ann *turns to go up drive, takes a couple of steps, sees* **Keller**, *and stops. He goes quietly on into house.*

Chris (*shaken, and therefore angered*)   Don't be an old lady.

Jim   He's come to take her home. What does that mean? (*To* **Ann**.) You know what that means. Fight it out with him some place else.

Ann (*comes back down toward* **Chris**)   I'll drive . . . him somewhere.

Chris (*goes to her*)   No.

Jim   Will you stop being an idiot?

Chris   Nobody's afraid of him here. Cut that out!

He starts for driveway, but is brought up short by **George**, *who enters there.* **George** *is* **Chris**'s *age, but a paler man, now on the edge of his self-restraint. He speaks quietly, as though afraid to find himself screaming.*

An instant's hesitation and **Chris** *steps up to him, hand extended, smiling.*

Chris   Helluva way to do; what're you sitting out there for?

George   Doctor said your mother isn't well, I –

Chris   So what? She'd want to see you, wouldn't she? We've been waiting for you all afternoon. (*He puts his hand on* **George***'s arm, but* **George** *pulls away, coming across toward* **Ann***.*)

Ann (*touching his collar*)   This is filthy, didn't you bring another shirt?

George *breaks away from her, and moves down, examining the yard. Door opens, and he turns rapidly, thinking it is* **Kate***, but it's* **Sue***. She looks at him; he turns away and moves to fence. He looks over it at his former home.* **Sue** *comes downstage.*

Sue (*annoyed*)   How about the beach, Jim?

Jim   Oh, it's too hot to drive.

Sue   How'd you get to the station – Zeppelin?

Chris   This is Mrs Bayliss, George. (*Calling, as* **George** *pays no attention, staring at house.*) George! (**George** *turns.*) Mrs Bayliss.

Sue   How do you do.

George (*removing his hat*)   You're the people who bought our house, aren't you?

Sue   That's right. Come and see what we did with it before you leave.

George (*walks down and away from her*)   I liked it the way it was.

Sue (*after a brief pause*)   He's frank, isn't he?

Jim (*pulling her off*)   See you later . . . Take it easy, fella. (*They exit.*)

Chris (*calling after them*)   Thanks for driving him! (*Turning to* **George***.*) How about some grape juice? Mother made it especially for you.

George (*with forced appreciation*)   Good old Kate, remembered my grape juice.

Chris   You drank enough of it in this house. How've you been, George? – Sit down.

George (*keeps moving*)   It takes me a minute. (*Looking around.*) It seems impossible.

Chris   What?

George   I'm back here.

Chris   Say, you've gotten a little nervous, haven't you?

George   Yeah, toward the end of the day. What're you, big executive now?

Chris   Just kind of medium. How's the law?

George   I don't know. When I was studying in the hospital it seemed sensible, but outside there doesn't seem to be much of a law. The trees got thick, didn't they? (*Points to stump.*) What's that?

Chris   Blew down last night. We had it there for Larry. You know.

George   Why, afraid you'll forget him?

Chris (*starts for* **George**)   Kind of a remark is that?

Ann (*breaking in, putting a restraining hand on* **Chris**)   When did you start wearing a hat?

George (*discovers hat in his hand*)   Today. From now on I decided to look like a lawyer, anyway. (*He holds it up to her.*) Don't you recognize it?

Ann   Why? Where – ?

George   Your father's – He asked me to wear it.

Ann   How is he?

George   He got smaller.

Ann   Smaller?

George Yeah, little. (*Holds out his hand to measure.*) He's a little man. That's what happens to suckers, you know. It's good I went to him in time – another year there'd be nothing left but his smell.

Chris What's the matter, George, what's the trouble?

George The trouble? The trouble is when you make suckers out of people once, you shouldn't try to do it twice.

Chris What does that mean?

George (*to **Ann***) You're not married yet, are you?

Ann George, will you sit down and stop – ?

George Are you married yet?

Ann No, I'm not married yet.

George You're not going to marry him.

Ann Why am I not going to marry him?

George Because his father destroyed your family.

Chris Now look, George . . .

George Cut it short, Chris. Tell her to come home with me. Let's not argue, you know what I've got to say.

Chris George, you don't want to be the voice of God, do you?

George I'm –

Chris That's been your trouble all your life, George, you dive into things. What kind of a statement is that to make? You're a big boy now.

George I'm a big boy now.

Chris Don't come bulling in here. If you've got something to say, be civilized about it.

George Don't civilize me!

Ann Shhh!

Chris (*ready to hit him*) Are you going to talk like a grown man or aren't you?

Ann (*quickly, to forestall an outburst*)   Sit down, dear. Don't be angry, what's the matter? (*He allows her to seat him, looking at her.*) Now what happened? You kissed me when I left, now you –

George (*breathlessly*)   My life turned upside down since then. I couldn't go back to work when you left. I wanted to go to Dad and tell him you were going to be married. It seemed impossible not to tell him. He loved you so much. (*He pauses.*) Annie – we did a terrible thing. We can never be forgiven. Not even to send him a card at Christmas. I didn't see him once since I got home from the war! Annie, you don't know what was done to that man. You don't know what happened.

Ann (*afraid*)   Of course I know.

George   You can't know, you wouldn't be here. Dad came to work that day. The night foreman came to him and showed him the cylinder heads . . . they were coming out of the process with defects. There was something wrong with the process. So Dad went directly to the phone and called here and told Joe to come down right away. But the morning passed. No sign of Joe. So Dad called again. By this time he had over a hundred defectives. The Army was screaming for stuff and Dad didn't have anything to ship. So Joe told him . . . on the phone he told him to weld, cover up the cracks in any way he could, and ship them out.

Chris   Are you through now?

George (*surging up at him*)   I'm not through now! (*Back to* **Ann**.) Dad was afraid. He wanted Joe there if he was going to do it. But Joe can't come down . . . He's sick. Sick! He suddenly gets the flu! Suddenly! But he promised to take responsibility. Do you understand what I'm saying? On the telephone you can't have responsibility! In a court you can always deny a phone call and that's exactly what he did. They knew he was a liar the first time, but in the appeal they believed that rotten lie and now Joe is a big shot and your father is the patsy. (*He gets up.*) Now what're you going to do? Eat his food, sleep in his bed? Answer me; what're you going to do?

Chris   What're you going to do, George?

George   He's too smart for me, I can't prove a phone call.

Chris   Then how dare you come in here with that rot?

Ann   George, the court –

George   The court didn't know your father! But you know him. You know in your heart Joe did it.

Chris (*whirling him around*)   Lower your voice or I'll throw you out of here!

George   She knows. She knows.

Chris (*to* **Ann**)   Get him out of here, Ann. Get him out of here.

Ann   George, I know everything you've said. Dad told that whole thing in court, and they –

George (*almost a scream*)   The court did not know him, Annie!

Ann   Shhh! – But he'll say anything, George. You know how quick he can lie.

George (*turning to* **Chris**, *with deliberation*)   I'll ask you something, and look me in the eye when you answer me.

Chris   I'll look you in the eye.

George   You know your father –

Chris   I know him well.

George   And he's the kind of boss to let a hundred and twenty-one cylinder heads be repaired and shipped out of his shop without even knowing about it?

Chris   He's that kind of boss.

George   And that's the same Joe Keller who never left his shop without first going around to see that all the lights were out.

Chris (*with growing anger*)   The same Joe Keller.

George   The same man who knows how many minutes a day his workers spend in the toilet.

Chris   The same man.

George   And my father, that frightened mouse who'd never buy a shirt without somebody along – that man would dare do such a thing on his own?

Chris   On his own. And because he's a frightened mouse this is another thing he'd do – throw the blame on somebody else because he's not man enough to take it himself. He tried it in court but it didn't work, but with a fool like you it works!

George   Oh, Chris, you're a liar to yourself!

Ann (*deeply shaken*)   Don't talk like that!

Chris (*sits facing* **George**)   Tell me, George. What happened? The court record was good enough for you all these years, why isn't it good now? Why did you believe it all these years?

George (*after a slight pause*)   Because you believed it . . . That's the truth, Chris. I believed everything, because I thought you did. But today I heard it from his mouth. From his mouth it's altogether different than the record. Anyone who knows him, and knows your father, will believe it from his mouth. Your Dad took everything we have. I can't beat that. But she's one item he's not going to grab. (*He turns to* **Ann**.) Get your things. Everything they have is covered with blood. You're not the kind of a girl who can live with that. Get your things.

Chris   Ann . . . you're not going to believe that, are you?

Ann (*goes to him*)   You know it's not true, don't you?

George   How can he tell you? It's his father. (*To* **Chris**.) None of these things ever even cross your mind?

Chris   Yes, they crossed my mind. Anything can cross your mind!

George   *He knows*, Annie. He knows!

Chris   The voice of God!

George   Then why isn't your name on the business? Explain that to her!

Chris What the hell has that got to do with – ?

George Annie, why isn't his name on it?

Chris Even when I don't own it!

George Who're you kidding? Who gets it when he dies? (*To* Ann.) Open your eyes, you know the both of them, isn't that the first thing they'd do, the way they love each other? – J.O. Keller and Son? (*Pause.* **Ann** *looks from him to* **Chris**.) I'll settle it. Do you want to settle it, or are you afraid to?

Chris What do you mean?

George Let me go up and talk to your father. In ten minutes you'll have the answer. Or are you afraid of the answer?

Chris I'm not afraid of the answer. I know the answer. But my mother isn't well and I don't want a fight here now.

George Let me go to him.

Chris You're not going to start a fight here now.

George (*to* **Ann**) What more do you want! (*There is a sound of footsteps in the house.*)

Ann (*turns her head suddenly toward house*) Someone's coming.

Chris (*to* **George**, *quietly*) You won't say anything now.

Ann You'll go soon. I'll call a cab.

George You're coming with me.

Ann And don't mention marriage, because we haven't told her yet.

George You're coming with me.

Ann You understand? Don't – George, you're not going to start anything now! (*She hears footsteps.*) Shhh!

Mother *enters on porch. She is dressed almost formally; her hair is fixed. They are all turned toward her. On seeing* **George** *she raises both hands, comes down toward him.*

Mother Georgie, Georgie.

George (*he has always liked her*)   Hello, Kate.

Mother (*cups his face in her hands*)   They made an old man out of you. (*Touches his hair.*) Look, you're gray.

George (*her pity, open and unabashed, reaches into him, and he smiles sadly*)   I know, I –

Mother   I told you when you went away, don't try for medals.

George (*laughs, tiredly*)   I didn't try, Kate. They made it very easy for me.

Mother (*actually angry*)   Go on. You're all alike. (*To* **Ann**.) Look at him, why did you say he's fine? He looks like a ghost.

George (*relishing her solicitude*)   I feel all right.

Mother   I'm sick to look at you. What's the matter with your mother, why don't she feed you?

Ann   He just hasn't any appetite.

Mother   If he ate in my house he'd have an appetite. (*To* **Ann**.) I pity your husband! (*To* **George**.) Sit down. I'll make you a sandwich.

George (*sits with an embarrassed laugh*)   I'm really not hungry.

Mother   Honest to God, it breaks my heart to see what happened to all the children. How we worked and planned for you, and you end up no better than us.

George (*with deep feeling for her*)   You . . . you haven't changed at all, you know that, Kate?

Mother   None of us changed, Georgie. We all love you. Joe was just talking about the day you were born and the water got shut off. People were carrying basins from a block away – a stranger would have thought the whole neighborhood was on fire! (*They laugh. She sees the juice. To* **Ann**.) Why didn't you give him some juice!

Ann (*defensively*)   I offered it to him.

Mother (*scoffingly*)   You offered it to him! (*Thrusting glass into* **George***'s hand.*) Give it to him! (*To* **George***, who is laughing.*) And now you're going to sit here and drink some juice . . . and look like something!

George (*sitting*)   Kate, I feel hungry already.

Chris (*proudly*)   She could turn Mahatma Gandhi into a heavyweight!

Mother (*to* **Chris***, with great energy*)   Listen, to hell with the restaurant! I got a ham in the icebox, and frozen strawberries, and avocados, and –

Ann   Swell, I'll help you!

George   The train leaves at eight-thirty, Ann.

Mother (*to* **Ann**)   You're leaving?

Chris   No, Mother, she's not –

Ann (*breaking through it, going to* **George**)   You hardly got here; give yourself a chance to get acquainted again.

Chris   Sure, you don't even know us any more.

Mother   Well, Chris, if they can't stay, don't –

Chris   No, it's just a question of George, Mother, he planned on –

George (*gets up politely, nicely, for* **Kate***'s sake*)   Now wait a minute, Chris . . .

Chris (*smiling and full of command, cutting him off*)   If you want to go, I'll drive you to the station now, but if you're staying, no arguments while you're here.

Mother (*at last confessing the tension*)   Why should he argue? (*She goes to him. With desperation and compassion, stroking his hair.*) Georgie and us have no argument. How could we have an argument, Georgie? We all got hit by the same lightning, how can you – ? Did you see what happened to Larry's tree, Georgie? (*She has taken his arm, and unwillingly he moves across stage* *with her.*) Imagine? While I was dreaming of him in the middle of the night, the wind came along and –

Lydia *enters on porch. As soon as she sees him:*

Lydia   Hey, Georgie! Georgie! Georgie! Georgie! Georgie! (*She comes down to him eagerly. She has a flowered hat in her hand, which* **Kate** *takes from her as she goes to* **George**.)

George (*as they shake hands eagerly, warmly*)   Hello, Laughy. What'd you do, grow?

Lydia   I'm a big girl now.

Mother   Look what she can do to a hat!

Ann (*to* **Lydia**, *admiring the hat*)   Did you make that?

Mother   In ten minutes! (*She puts it on.*)

Lydia (*fixing it on her head*)   I only rearranged it.

George   You still make your own clothes?

Chris (*of* **Mother**)   Ain't she classy! All she needs now is a Russian wolfhound.

Mother (*moving her head*)   It feels like somebody is sitting on my head.

Ann   No, it's beautiful, Kate.

Mother (*kisses* **Lydia**. *To* **George**)   She's a genius! You should've married her. (*They laugh.*) This one can feed you!

Lydia (*strangely embarrassed*)   Oh, stop that, Kate.

George (*to* **Lydia**)   Didn't I hear you had a baby?

Mother   You don't hear so good. She's got three babies.

George (*a little hurt by it – to* **Lydia**)   No kidding, three?

Lydia   Yeah, it was one, two, three – You've been away a long time, Georgie.

George   I'm beginning to realize.

Mother (*to* **Chris** *and* **George**)   The trouble with you kids is you *think* too much.

Lydia   Well, we think, too.

Mother   Yes, but not all the time.

George (*with almost obvious envy*)   They never took Frank, heh?

Lydia (*a little apologetically*)   No, he was always one year ahead of the draft.

Mother   It's amazing. When they were calling boys twenty-seven Frank was just twenty-eight, when they made it twenty-eight he was just twenty-nine. That's why he took up astrology. It's all in when you were born, it just goes to show.

Chris   What does it go to show?

Mother (*to* **Chris**)   Don't be so intelligent. Some superstitions are very nice! (*To* **Lydia**.) Did he finish Larry's horoscope?

Lydia   I'll ask him now, I'm going in. (*To* **George**, *a little sadly, almost embarrassed.*) Would you like to see my babies? Come on.

George   I don't think so, Lydia.

Lydia (*understanding*)   All right. Good luck to you, George.

George   Thanks. And to you . . . And Frank. (*She smiles at him, turns and goes off to her house.* **George** *stands staring after her.*)

Lydia (*as she runs off*)   Oh, Frank!

Mother (*reading his thoughts*)   She got pretty, heh?

George (*sadly*)   Very pretty.

Mother (*as a reprimand*)   She's beautiful, you damned fool!

George (*looks around longingly; and softly, with a catch in his throat*) She makes it seem so nice around here.

Mother (*shaking her finger at him*)   Look what happened to you because you wouldn't listen to me! I told you to marry that girl and stay out of the war!

George (*laughs at himself*)   She used to laugh too much.

Mother   And you didn't laugh enough. While you were getting mad about Fascism Frank was getting into her bed.

George (*to* **Chris**)   He won the war, Frank.

Chris   All the battles.

Mother (*in pursuit of this mood*)   The day they started the draft, Georgie, I told you you loved that girl.

Chris (*laughs*)   And truer love hath no man!

Mother   I'm smarter than any of you.

George (*laughing*)   She's wonderful!

Mother   And now you're going to listen to me, George. You had big principles, Eagle Scouts the three of you; so now I got a tree, and this one – (*Indicating* **Chris**.) when the weather gets bad he can't stand on his feet; and that big dope – (*Pointing to* **Lydia**'s *house*.) next door who never reads anything but Andy Gump has three children and his house paid off. Stop being a philosopher, and look after yourself. Like Joe was just saying – you move back here, he'll help you get set, and I'll find you a girl and put a smile on your face.

George   Joe? Joe wants me here?

Ann (*eagerly*)   He asked me to tell you, and I think it's a good idea.

Mother   Certainly. Why must you make believe you hate us? Is that another principle? – that you have to hate us? You don't hate us, George, I know you, you can't fool me, I diapered you. (*Suddenly, to* **Ann**.) You remember Mr Marcy's daughter?

Ann (*laughing, to* **George**)   She's got you hooked already! (**George** *laughs, is excited*.)

Mother   You look her over, George; you'll see she's the most beautiful –

Chris   She's got warts, George.

Mother (*to* **Chris**)   She hasn't got warts! (*To* **George**.) So the girl has a little beauty mark on her chin –

Chris   And two on her nose.

Mother   You remember. Her father's the retired police inspector.

Chris   Sergeant, George.

Mother   He's a very kind man!

Chris   He looks like a gorilla.

Mother (*to* **George**)   He never shot anybody.

They all burst out laughing, as **Keller** *appears in doorway.*

George *rises abruptly and stares at* **Keller**, *who comes rapidly down to him.*

Keller (*the laughter stops. With strained joviality*)   Well! Look who's here! (*Extending his hand.*) Georgie, good to see ya.

George (*shaking hands – somberly*)   How're you, Joe?

Keller   So-so. Gettin' old. You comin' out to dinner with us?

George   No, got to be back in New York.

Ann   I'll call a cab for you. (*She goes up into the house.*)

Keller   Too bad you can't stay, George. Sit down. (*To* **Mother**.) He looks fine.

Mother   He looks terrible.

Keller   That's what I said, you look terrible, George. (*They laugh.*) I wear the pants and she beats me with the belt.

George   I saw your factory on the way from the station. It looks like General Motors.

Keller   I wish it was General Motors, but it ain't. Sit down, George. Sit down. (*Takes cigar out of his pocket.*) So you finally went to see your father, I hear?

George   Yes, this morning. What kind of stuff do you make now?

Keller   Oh, little of everything. Pressure cookers, an assembly for washing machines. Got a nice, flexible plant now. So how'd you find Dad? Feel all right?

George (*searching* **Keller**, *speaking indecisively*)   No, he's not well, Joe.

Keller (*lighting his cigar*)   Not his heart again, is it?

George   It's everything, Joe. It's his soul.

Keller (*blowing out smoke*)   Uh huh –

Chris   How about seeing what they did with your house?

Keller   Leave him be.

George (*to* **Chris**, *indicating* **Keller**)   I'd like to talk to him.

Keller   Sure, he just got here. That's the way they do, George. A little man makes a mistake and they hang him by the thumbs; the big ones become ambassadors. I wish you'd-a told me you were going to see Dad.

George (*studying him*)   I didn't know you were interested.

Keller   In a way, I am. I would like him to know, George, that as far as I'm concerned, any time he wants, he's got a place with me. I would like him to know that.

George   He hates your guts, Joe. Don't you know that?

Keller   I imagined it. But that can change, too.

Mother   Steve was never like that.

George   He's like that now. He'd like to take every man who made money in the war and put him up against a wall.

Chris   He'll need a lot of bullets.

George   And he'd better not get any.

Keller   That's a sad thing to hear.

George (*with bitterness dominant*)   Why? What'd you expect him to think of you?

Keller (*the force of his nature rising, but under control*)   I'm sad to see he hasn't changed. As long as I know him, twenty-five years, the man never learned how to take the blame. You know that, George.

George (*he does*)   Well, I –

Keller   But you do know it. Because the way you come in here you don't look like you remember it. I mean like in nineteen thirty-seven when we had the shop on Flood Street. And he damn near blew us all up with that heater he left burning for two days without water. He wouldn't admit that was his fault, either. I had to fire a mechanic to save his face. You remember that.

George   Yes, but –

Keller   I'm just mentioning it, George. Because this is just another one of a lot of things. Like when he gave Frank that money to invest in oil stock.

George (*distressed*)   I know that, I –

Keller (*driving in, but restrained*)   But it's good to remember those things, kid. The way he cursed Frank because the stock went down. Was that Frank's fault? To listen to him Frank was a swindler. And all the man did was give him a bad tip.

George (*gets up, moves away*)   I know those things . . .

Keller   Then remember them, remember them. (**Ann** *comes out of house.*) There are certain men in the world who rather see everybody hung before they'll take blame. You understand me, George?

They stand facing each other, **George** *trying to judge him.*

Ann (*coming downstage*)   The cab's on its way. Would you like to wash?

Mother (*with the thrust of hope*)   Why must he go? Make the midnight, George.

Keller Sure, you'll have dinner with us!

Ann How about it? Why not? We're eating at the lake, we could have a swell time.

A long pause, as **George** *looks at* **Ann**, **Chris**, **Keller**, *then back to her.*

George All right.

Mother Now you're talking.

Chris I've got a shirt that'll go right with that suit.

Mother Size fifteen and a half, right, George?

George Is Lydia – ? I mean – Frank and Lydia coming?

Mother I'll get you a date that'll make her look like a – (*She starts upstage.*)

George (*laughing*) No, I don't want a date.

Chris I know somebody just for you! Charlotte Tanner! (*He starts for the house.*)

Keller Call Charlotte, that's right.

Mother Sure, call her up. (**Chris** *goes into house.*)

Ann You go up and pick out a shirt and tie.

George (*stops, looks around at them and the place*) I never felt at home anywhere but here. I feel so – (*He nearly laughs, and turns away from them.*) Kate, you look so young, you know? You didn't change at all. It . . . rings an old bell. (*Turns to* **Keller**.) You too, Joe, you're amazingly the same. The whole atmosphere is.

Keller Say, I ain't got time to get sick.

Mother He hasn't been laid up in fifteen years.

Keller Except my flu during the war.

Mother Huhh?

Keller My flu, when I was sick during . . . the war.

Mother   Well, sure . . . (*To* **George**.) I mean except for that flu. (**George** *stands perfectly still.*) Well, it slipped my mind, don't look at me that way. He wanted to go to the shop but he couldn't lift himself off the bed. I thought he had pneumonia.

George   Why did you say he's never – ?

Keller   I know how you feel, kid, I'll never forgive myself. If I could've gone in that day I'd never allow Dad to touch those heads.

George   She said you've never been sick.

Mother   I said he was sick, George.

George (*going to* **Ann**)   Ann, didn't you hear her say – ?

Mother   Do you remember every time you were sick?

George   I'd remember pneumonia. Especially if I got it just the day my partner was going to patch up cylinder heads . . . What happened that day, Joe?

Frank *enters briskly from driveway, holding Larry's horoscope in his hand. He comes to* **Kate**.

Frank   Kate! Kate!

Mother   Frank, did you see George?

Frank (*extending his hand*)   Lydia told me, I'm glad to . . . you'll have to pardon me. (*Pulling* **Mother** *over.*) I've got something amazing for you, Kate, I finished Larry's horoscope.

Mother   You'd be interested in this, George. It's wonderful the way he can understand the –

Chris (*entering from house*)   George, the girl's on the phone –

Mother (*desperately*)   He finished Larry's horoscope!

Chris   Frank, can't you pick a better time than this?

Frank   The greatest men who ever lived believed in the stars!

Chris   Stop filling her head with that junk!

Frank   Is it junk to feel that there's a greater power than ourselves? I've studied the stars of his life! I won't argue with you, I'm telling you. Somewhere in this world your brother is alive!

Mother (*instantly to* **Chris**)   Why isn't it possible?

Chris   Because it's insane.

Frank   Just a minute now. I'll tell you something and you can do as you please. Just let me say it. He was supposed to have died on November twenty-fifth. But November twenty-fifth was his favorable day.

Chris   Mother!

Mother   Listen to him!

Frank   It was a day when everything good was shining on him, the kind of day he should've married on. You can laugh at a lot of it, I can understand you laughing. But the odds are a million to one that a man won't die on his favorable day. That's known, that's known, Chris!

Mother   Why isn't it possible, why isn't it possible, Chris!

George (*to* **Ann**)   Don't you understand what she's saying? She just told you to go. What are you waiting for now?

Chris   Nobody can tell her to go. (*A car horn is heard.*)

Mother (*to* **Frank**)   Thank you, darling, for your trouble. Will you tell him to wait, Frank?

Frank (*as he goes*)   Sure thing.

Mother (*calling out*)   They'll be right out, driver!

Chris   She's not leaving, Mother.

George   You heard her say it, he's never been sick!

Mother   He misunderstood me, Chris! (**Chris** *looks at her, struck.*)

George (*to* **Ann**)   He simply told your father to kill pilots, and covered himself in bed!

Chris   You'd better answer him, Annie. Answer him.

Mother   I packed your bag, darling.

Chris   What?

Mother   I packed your bag. All you've got to do is close it.

Ann   I'm not closing anything. He asked me here and I'm staying till he tells me to go. (*To* **George**.) Till Chris tells me!

Chris   That's all! Now get out of here, George!

Mother (*to* **Chris**)   But if that's how he feels –

Chris   That's all, nothing more till Christ comes, about the case or Larry as long as I'm here! (*To* **George**.) Now get out of here, George!

George (*to* **Ann**)   You tell me. I want to hear you tell me.

Ann   Go, George!

They disappear up the driveway, **Ann** *saying, 'Don't take it that way, Georgie! Please don't take it that way.'*

Chris (*turning to his mother*)   What do you mean, you packed her bag? How dare you pack her bag?

Mother   Chris –

Chris   How dare you pack her bag?

Mother   She doesn't belong here.

Chris   Then I don't belong here.

Mother   She's Larry's girl.

Chris   And I'm his brother and he's dead, and I'm marrying his girl.

Mother   Never, never in this world!

Keller   You lost your mind?

Mother   You have nothing to say!

Keller (*cruelly*)   I got plenty to say. Three and a half years you been talking like a maniac –

Mother *smashes him across the face.*

Mother   Nothing. You have nothing to say. Now I say. He's coming back, and everybody has got to wait.

Chris   Mother, Mother –

Mother   Wait, wait –

Chris   How long? How long?

Mother (*rolling out of her*)   Till he comes; forever and ever till he comes!

Chris (*as an ultimatum*)   Mother, I'm going ahead with it.

Mother   Chris, I've never said no to you in my life, now I say no!

Chris   You'll never let him go till I do it.

Mother   I'll never let him go and you'll never let him go!

Chris   I've let him go. I've let him go a long –

Mother (*with no less force, but turning from him*)   Then let your father go. (*Pause.* **Chris** *stands transfixed.*)

Keller   She's out of her mind.

Mother   Altogether! (*To* **Chris**, *but not facing them.*) Your brother's alive, darling, because if he's dead, your father killed him. Do you understand me now? As long as you live, that boy is alive. God does not let a son be killed by his father. Now you see, don't you? Now you see. (*Beyond control, she hurries up and into house.*)

Keller (**Chris** *has not moved. He speaks insinuatingly, questioningly*) She's out of her mind.

Chris (*in a broken whisper*)   Then . . . you did it?

Keller (*with the beginning of plea in his voice*)   He never flew a P-40 –

Chris (*struck; deadly*)   But the others.

Keller (*insistently*)   She's out of her mind. (*He takes a step toward* **Chris**, *pleadingly.*)

Chris (*unyielding*)   Dad . . . you did it?

Keller   He never flew a P-40, what's the matter with you?

Chris (*still asking, and saying*)   Then you did it. To the others.

Both hold their voices down.

Keller (*afraid of him, his deadly insistence*)   What's the matter with you? What the hell is the matter with you?

Chris (*quietly, incredibly*)   How could you do that? How?

Keller   What's the matter with you!

Chris   Dad . . . Dad, you killed twenty-one men!

Keller   What, killed?

Chris   You killed them, you murdered them.

Keller (*as though throwing his whole nature open before* **Chris**) How could I kill anybody?

Chris   Dad! Dad!

Keller (*trying to hush him*)   I didn't kill anybody!

Chris   Then explain it to me. What did you do? Explain it to me or I'll tear you to pieces!

Keller (*horrified at his overwhelming fury*)   Don't, Chris, don't –

Chris   I want to know what you did, now what did you do? You had a hundred and twenty cracked engine-heads, now what did you do?

Keller   If you're going to hang me then I –

Chris   I'm listening. God Almighty, I'm listening!

Keller (*their movements now are those of subtle pursuit and escape.* **Keller** *keeps a step out of* **Chris**'s *range as he talks*)   You're a boy, what could I do! I'm in business, a man is in business; a hundred and twenty cracked, you're out of business; you got a process, the process don't work you're out of business; you don't know how to operate, your stuff is no good; they close you up, they tear up your contracts, what the hell's it to them? You lay forty years into a business and they knock you out in five minutes, what could I do, let them take forty years, let them take my life away? (*His voice cracking.*) I never thought they'd install them. I swear to God. I thought they'd stop 'em before anybody took off.

Chris   Then why'd you ship them out?

Keller   By the time they could spot them I thought I'd have the process going again, and I could show them they needed me and they'd let it go by. But weeks passed and I got no kickback, so I was going to tell them.

Chris   Then why didn't you tell them?

Keller   It was too late. The paper, it was all over the front page, twenty-one went down, it was too late. They came with handcuffs into the shop, what could I do? (*He sits on bench.*) Chris . . . Chris, I did it for you, it was a chance and I took it for you. I'm sixty-one years old, when would I have another chance to make something for you? Sixty-one years old you don't get another chance, do ya?

Chris   You even knew they wouldn't hold up in the air.

Keller   I didn't say that.

Chris   But you were going to warn them not to use them –

Keller   But that don't mean –

Chris   It means you knew they'd crash.

Keller   It don't mean that.

Chris   Then you *thought* they'd crash.

Keller   I was afraid maybe –

Chris   You were afraid maybe! God in heaven, what kind of a man are you? Kids were hanging in the air by those heads. You knew that!

Keller   For you, a business for you!

Chris (*with burning fury*)   For me! Where do you live, where have you come from? For me! – I was dying every day and you were killing my boys and you did it for me? What the hell do you think I was thinking of, the goddam business? Is that as far as your mind can see, the business? What is that, the world – the business? What the hell do you mean, you did it for me? Don't you have a country? Don't you live in the world? What the hell are you? You're not even an animal, no animal kills his own, what are you? What must I do to you? I ought to tear the tongue out of your mouth, what must I do? (*With his fist he pounds down upon his father's shoulder. He stumbles away, covering his face as he weeps.*) What must I do, Jesus God, what must I do?

Keller   Chris . . . My Chris . . .

Curtain.

Act Three

Two o'clock the following morning, **Mother** *is discovered on the rise, rocking ceaselessly in a chair, staring at her thoughts. It is an intense, slight, sort of rocking. A light shows from upstairs bedroom, lower floor windows being dark. The moon is strong and casts its bluish light.*

Presently **Jim***, dressed in jacket and hat, appears, and seeing her, goes up beside her.*

Jim   Any news?

Mother   No news.

Jim (*gently*)   You can't sit up all night, dear, why don't you go to bed?

Mother   I'm waiting for Chris. Don't worry about me, Jim, I'm perfectly all right.

Jim   But it's almost two o'clock.

Mother   I can't sleep. (*Slight pause.*) You had an emergency?

Jim (*tiredly*)   Somebody had a headache and thought he was dying. (*Slight pause.*) Half of my patients are quite mad. Nobody realizes how many people are walking around loose, and they're cracked as coconuts. Money. Money – money – money – money. You say it long enough it doesn't mean anything. (*She smiles, makes a silent laugh.*) Oh, how I'd love to be around when that happens!

Mother (*shaking her head*)   You're so childish, Jim! Sometimes you are.

Jim (*looks at her a moment*)   Kate. (*Pause.*) What happened?

Mother   I told you. He had an argument with Joe. Then he got in the car and drove away.

Jim   What kind of an argument?

Mother   An argument, Joe . . . He was crying like a child, before.

Jim   They argued about Ann?

Mother (*after slight hesitation*)   No, not Ann. Imagine? (*Indicates lighted window above.*) She hasn't come out of that room since he left. All night in that room.

Jim (*looks at window, then at her*)   What'd Joe do, tell him?

Mother (*stops rocking*)   Tell him what?

Jim   Don't be afraid, Kate, I know. I've always known.

Mother   How?

Jim   It occurred to me a long time ago.

Mother   I always had the feeling that in the back of his head, Chris . . . almost knew. I didn't think it would be such a shock.

Jim (*gets up*)   Chris would never know how to live with a thing like that. It takes a certain talent – for lying. You have it, and I do. But not him.

Mother   What do you mean . . . He's not coming back?

Jim   Oh, no, he'll come back. We all come back, Kate. These private little revolutions always die. The compromise is always made. In a peculiar way. Frank is right – every man does have a star. The star of one's honesty. And you spend your life groping for it, but once it's out it never lights again. I don't think he went very far. He probably just wanted to be alone to watch his star go out.

Mother   Just as long as he comes back.

Jim   I wish he wouldn't, Kate. One year I simply took off, went to New Orleans; for two months I lived on bananas and milk, and studied a certain disease. It was beautiful. And then she came, and she cried. And I went back home with her. And now I live in the usual darkness; I can't find myself; it's even hard sometimes to remember the kind of man I wanted to be. I'm a good husband; Chris is a good son – he'll come back.

Keller *comes out on porch in dressing gown and slippers. He goes upstage – to alley.* **Jim** *goes to him.*

Jim   I have a feeling he's in the park. I'll look around for him. Put her to bed, Joe; this is no good for what she's got. (**Jim** *exits up driveway.*)

Keller (*coming down*)   What does he want here?

Mother   His friend is not home.

Keller (*comes down to her. His voice is husky*)   I don't like him mixing in so much.

Mother   It's too late, Joe. He knows.

Keller (*apprehensively*)   How does he know?

Mother   He guessed a long time ago.

Keller   I don't like that.

Mother (*laughs dangerously, quietly into the line*)   What you don't like.

Keller   Yeah, what I don't like.

Mother   You can't bull yourself through this one, Joe, you better be smart now. This thing – this thing is not over yet.

Keller (*indicating lighted window above*)   And what is she doing up there? She don't come out of the room.

Mother   I don't know, what is she doing? Sit down, stop being mad. You want to live? You better figure out your life.

Keller   She don't know, does she?

Mother   She saw Chris storming out of here. It's one and one – she knows how to add.

Keller   Maybe I ought to talk to her?

Mother   Don't ask me, Joe.

Keller (*almost an outburst*)   Then who do I ask? But I don't think she'll do anything about it.

Mother   You're asking me again.

Keller   I'm askin' you. What am I, a stranger? I thought I had a family here. What happened to my family?

Mother   You've got a family. I'm simply telling you that I have no strength to think any more.

Keller   You have no strength. The minute there's trouble you have no strength.

Mother   Joe, you're doing the same thing again; all your life whenever there's trouble you yell at me and you think that settles it.

Keller   Then what do I do? Tell me, talk to me, what do I do?

Mother   Joe . . . I've been thinking this way. If he comes back –

Keller   What do you mean 'if'? He's comin' back!

Mother   I think if you sit him down and you – explain yourself. I mean you ought to make it clear to him that you know you did a terrible thing. (*Not looking into his eyes.*) I mean if he saw that you realize what you did. You see?

Keller   What ice does that cut?

Mother (*a little fearfully*)   I mean if you told him that you want to pay for what you did.

Keller (*sensing . . . quietly*)   How can I pay?

Mother   Tell him – you're willing to go to prison. (*Pause.*)

Keller (*struck, amazed*)   I'm willing to – ?

Mother (*quickly*)   You wouldn't go, he wouldn't ask you to go. But if you told him you wanted to, if he could feel that you wanted to pay, maybe he would forgive you.

Keller   He would forgive me! For what?

Mother   Joe, you know what I mean.

Keller   I don't know what you mean! You wanted money, so I made money. What must I be forgiven? You wanted money, didn't you?

Mother   I didn't want it that way.

Keller   I didn't want it that way, either! What difference is it what you want? I spoiled the both of you. I should've put him out when he was ten like I was put out, and make him earn his keep. Then he'd know how a buck is made in this world. Forgiven! I could live on a quarter a day myself, but I got a family so I –

Mother   Joe, Joe . . . It don't excuse it that you did it for the family.

Keller   It's got to excuse it!

Mother   There's something bigger than the family to him.

Keller   Nothin' is bigger!

Mother   There is to him.

Keller   There's nothin' he could do that I wouldn't forgive. Because he's my son. Because I'm his father and he's my son.

Mother   Joe, I tell you –

Keller   Nothin's bigger than that. And you're goin' to tell him, you understand? I'm his father and he's my son, and if there's something bigger than that I'll put a bullet in my head!

Mother   You stop that!

Keller   You heard me. Now you know what to tell him. (*Pause. He moves from her – halts.*) But he wouldn't put me away though . . . He wouldn't do that . . . Would he?

Mother   He loved you, Joe, you broke his heart.

Keller   But to put me away . . .

Mother   I don't know. I'm beginning to think we don't really know him. They say in the war he was such a killer. Here he was always afraid of mice. I don't know him. I don't know what he'll do.

Keller   Goddam, if Larry was alive he wouldn't act like this. He understood the way the world is made. He listened to me. To him the world had a forty-foot front, it ended at the building line. This one, everything bothers him. You make a deal, overcharge two cents, and his hair falls out. He don't understand money. Too easy, it came too easy. Yes, sir. Larry. That was a boy we lost. Larry. Larry. (*He slumps on chair in front of her.*) What am I gonna do, Kate?

Mother   Joe, Joe, please . . . You'll be all right, nothing is going to happen.

Keller (*desperately, lost*)   For you, Kate, for both of you, that's all I ever lived for . . .

Mother   I know, darling, I know. (**Ann** *enters from house. They say nothing, waiting for her to speak.*)

Ann   Why do you stay up? I'll tell you when he comes.

Keller (*rises, goes to her*)   You didn't eat supper, did you? (*To* **Mother**.) Why don't you make her something?

Mother   Sure, I'll –

Ann   Never mind, Kate, I'm all right. (*They are unable to speak to each other.*) There's something I want to tell you. (*She starts, then halts.*) I'm not going to do anything about it.

Mother   She's a good girl! (*To* **Keller**.) You see? She's a –

Ann   I'll do nothing about Joe, but you're going to do something for me. (*Directly to* **Mother**.) You made Chris feel guilty with me. Whether you wanted to or not, you've crippled him in front of me. I'd like you to tell him that Larry is dead and that you know it. You understand me? I'm not going out of here alone. There's no life for me that way. I want you to set him free. And then I promise you, everything will end, and we'll go away, and that's all.

Keller   You'll do that. You'll tell him.

Ann   I know what I'm asking, Kate. You had two sons. But you've only got one now.

Keller   You'll tell him.

Ann   And you've got to say it to him so he knows you mean it.

Mother   My dear, if the boy was dead, it wouldn't depend on my words to make Chris know it . . . The night he gets into your bed, his heart will dry up. Because he knows and you know. To his dying day he'll wait for his brother! No, my dear, no such thing. You're going in the morning, and you're going alone. That's your life, that's your lonely life. (*She goes to porch, and starts in.*)

Ann   Larry is dead, Kate.

Mother (*she stops*)   Don't speak to me.

Ann   I said he's dead. I know! He crashed off the coast of China November twenty-fifth! His engine didn't fail him. But he died. I know . . .

Mother   How did he die? You're lying to me. If you know, how did he die?

Ann   I loved him. You know I loved him. Would I have looked at anyone else if I wasn't sure? That's enough for you.

Mother (*moving on her*)   What's enough for me? What're you talking about? (*She grasps **Ann**'s wrists.*)

Ann   You're hurting my wrists.

Mother   What are you talking about! (*Pause. She stares at **Ann** a moment, then turns and goes to **Keller**.*)

Ann   Joe, go in the house.

Keller   Why should I –

Ann   Please go.

Keller   Lemme know when he comes. (**Keller** *goes into house.*)

Mother (*as she sees **Ann** taking a letter from her pocket*)   What's that?

Ann   Sit down. (**Mother** *moves left to chair, but does not sit.*) First you've got to understand. When I came, I didn't have any idea that Joe – I had nothing against him or you. I came to get married. I hoped . . . So I didn't bring this to hurt you. I thought I'd show it to you only if there was no other way to settle Larry in your mind.

Mother   Larry? (*Snatches letter from* **Ann***'s hand.*)

Ann   He wrote it to me just before he – (**Mother** *opens and begins to read letter.*) I'm not trying to hurt you, Kate. You're making me do this, now remember you're – Remember. I've been so lonely, Kate . . . I can't leave here alone again. (*A long, low moan comes from* **Mother***'s throat as she reads.*) You made me show it to you. You wouldn't believe me. I told you a hundred times, why wouldn't you believe me!

Mother   Oh, my God . . .

Ann (*with pity and fear*)   Kate, please, please . . .

Mother   My God, my God . . .

Ann   Kate, dear, I'm so sorry . . . I'm so sorry.

Chris *enters from driveway. He seems exhausted.*

Chris   What's the matter – ?

Ann   Where were you? . . . You're all perspired. (**Mother** *doesn't move.*) Where were you?

Chris   Just drove around a little. I thought you'd be gone.

Ann   Where do I go? I have nowhere to go.

Chris (*to* **Mother**)   Where's Dad?

Ann   Inside lying down.

Chris   Sit down, both of you. I'll say what there is to say.

Mother   I didn't hear the car . . .

Chris   I left it in the garage.

Mother   Jim is out looking for you.

Chris   Mother . . . I'm going away. There are a couple of firms in Cleveland, I think I can get a place. I mean, I'm going away for good. (*To* **Ann** *alone.*) I know what you're thinking, Annie. It's true. I'm yellow. I was made yellow in this house because I suspected my father and I did nothing about it, but if I knew that night when I came home what I know now, he'd be in the district attorney's office by this time, and I'd have brought him there. Now if I look at him, all I'm able to do is cry.

Mother   What are you talking about? What else can you do?

Chris   I could jail him! I could jail him, if I were human any more. But I'm like everybody else now. I'm practical now. You made me practical.

Mother   But you have to be.

Chris   The cats in that alley are practical, the bums who ran away when we were fighting were practical. Only the dead ones weren't practical. But now I'm practical, and I spit on myself. I'm going away. I'm going now.

Ann (*going up to him*)   I'm coming with you.

Chris   No, Ann.

Ann   Chris, I don't ask you to do anything about Joe.

Chris   You do, you do.

Ann   I swear I never will.

Chris   In your heart you always will.

Ann   Then do what you have to do!

Chris   Do what? What is there to do? I've looked all night for a reason to make him suffer.

Ann   There's reason, there's reason!

Chris   What? Do I raise the dead when I put him behind bars? Then what'll I do it for? We used to shoot a man who acted like a dog, but honor was real there, you were protecting something. But here? This is the land of the great big dogs, you don't love a man here, you eat him! That's the principle; the only one we live by – it just happened to kill a few people this time, that's all. The world's that way, how can I take it out on him? What sense does that make? This is a zoo, a zoo!

Ann (*to* **Mother**)   You know what he's got to do! Tell him!

Mother   Let him go.

Ann   I won't let him go. You'll tell him what he's got to do . . .

Mother   Annie!

Ann   Then I will!

Keller *enters from house.* **Chris** *sees him, goes down near arbor.*

Keller   What's the matter with you? I want to talk to you.

Chris   I've got nothing to say to you.

Keller (*taking his arm*)   I want to talk to you!

Chris (*pulling violently away from him*)   Don't do that, Dad. I'm going to hurt you if you do that. There's nothing to say, so say it quick.

Keller   Exactly what's the matter? What's the matter? You got too much money? Is that what bothers you?

Chris (*with an edge of sarcasm*)   It bothers me.

Keller   If you can't get used to it, then throw it away. You hear me? Take every cent and give it to charity, throw it in the sewer. Does that settle it? In the sewer, that's all. You think I'm kidding? I'm tellin' you what to do, if it's dirty then burn it. It's your money, that's not my money. I'm a dead man, I'm an old dead man, nothing's mine. Well, talk to me! What do you want to do!

Chris   It's not what I want to do. It's what you want to do.

Keller   What should I want to do? (**Chris** *is silent.*) Jail? You want me to go to jail? If you want me to go, say so! Is that where I belong? Then tell me so! (*Slight pause.*) What's the matter, why can't you tell me? (*Furiously.*) You say everything else to me, say that! (*Slight pause.*) I'll tell you why you can't say it. Because you know I don't belong there. Because you know! (*With growing emphasis and passion, and a persistent tone of desperation.*) Who worked for nothin' in that war? When they work for nothin', I'll work for nothin'. Did they ship a gun or a truck outa Detroit before they got their price? Is that clean? It's dollars and cents, nickels and dimes; war and peace, it's nickels and dimes, what's clean? Half the goddam country is gotta go if I go! That's why you can't tell me.

Chris   That's exactly why.

Keller   Then . . . why am I bad?

Chris   I know you're no worse than most men but I thought you were better. I never saw you as a man. I saw you as my father. (*Almost breaking.*) I can't look at you this way, I can't look at myself!

He turns away, unable to face **Keller**. **Ann** *goes quickly to* **Mother**, *takes letter from her and starts for* **Chris**. **Mother** *instantly rushes to intercept her.*

Mother   Give me that!

Ann   He's going to read it! (*She thrusts letter into* **Chris**'s *hand.*) Larry. He wrote it to me the day he died.

Keller   Larry!

Mother   Chris, it's not for you. (*He starts to read.*) Joe . . . go away . . .

Keller (*mystified, frightened*)   Why'd she say, Larry, what – ?

Mother (*desperately pushes him toward alley, glancing at* **Chris**) Go to the street, Joe, go to the street! (*She comes down beside* **Keller**.) Don't, Chris . . . (*Pleading from her whole soul.*) Don't tell him.

Chris (*quietly*)   Three and one half years . . . talking, talking. Now you tell me what you must do . . . This is how he died, now tell me where you belong.

Keller (*pleading*)   Chris, a man can't be a Jesus in this world!

Chris   I know all about the world. I know the whole crap story. Now listen to this, and tell me what a man's got to be! (*Reads.*) 'My dear Ann: . . . ' You listening? He wrote this the day he died. Listen, don't cry . . . Listen! 'My dear Ann: It is impossible to put down the things I feel. But I've got to tell you something. Yesterday they flew in a load of papers from the States and I read about Dad and your father being convicted. I can't express myself. I can't tell you how I feel – I can't bear to live any more. Last night I circled the base for twenty minutes before I could bring myself in. How could he have done that? Every day three or four men never come back and he sits back there doing business . . . I don't know how to tell you what I feel . . . I can't face anybody . . . I'm going out on a mission in a few minutes. They'll probably report me missing. If they do, I want you to know that you mustn't wait for me. I tell you, Ann, if I had him there now I could kill him – ' (**Keller** *grabs letter from* **Chris**'s *hand and reads it. After a long pause.*) Now blame the world. Do you understand that letter?

Keller (*speaking almost inaudibly*)   I think I do. Get the car. I'll put on my jacket. (*He turns and starts slowly for the house.* **Mother** *rushes to intercept him.*)

Mother   Why are you going? You'll sleep, why are you going?

Keller   I can't sleep here. I'll feel better if I go.

Mother   You're so foolish. Larry was your son too, wasn't he? You know he'd never tell you to do this.

Keller (*looking at letter in his hand*)   Then what is this if it isn't telling me? Sure, he was my son. But I think to him they were all my sons. And I guess they were, I guess they were. I'll be right down. (*Exits into house.*)

Mother (*to* **Chris**, *with determination*)   You're not going to take him!

Chris   I'm taking him.

Mother   It's up to you, if you tell him to stay he'll stay. Go and tell him!

Chris   Nobody could stop him now.

Mother   You'll stop him! How long will he live in prison? Are you trying to kill him?

Chris (*holding out letter*)   I thought you read this!

Mother (*of Larry, the letter*)   The war is over! Didn't you hear? It's over!

Chris   Then what was Larry to you? A stone that fell into the water? It's not enough for him to be sorry. Larry didn't kill himself to make you and Dad sorry.

Mother   What more can we be!

Chris   You can be better! Once and for all you can know there's a universe of people outside and you're responsible to it, and unless you know that, you threw away your son because that's why he died.

A shot is heard in the house. They stand frozen for a brief second. **Chris** *starts for porch, pauses at step, turns to* **Ann**.

Chris   Find Jim! (*He goes on into the house and* **Ann** *runs up driveway.* **Mother** *stands alone, transfixed.*)

Mother (*softly, almost moaning*)   Joe . . . Joe . . . Joe . . . Joe . . . (**Chris** *comes out of house, down to* **Mother**'s *arms.*)

Chris (*almost crying*)   Mother, I didn't mean to –

Mother   Don't dear. Don't take it on yourself. Forget now. Live. (**Chris** *stirs as if to answer.*) Shhh . . . (*She puts his arms down gently and moves toward porch.*) Shhh . . . (*As she reaches porch steps she begins sobbing.*)

Curtain.

Notes

in the Roman Catholic Church, Jesus, his mother the
Virgin Mary, and his human father figure, Joseph.

49   *But if Chris wants to put on the hair shirt let him take off his
      broadcloth*: a hair shirt is traditionally a means of religious
      mortification by wearing undergarments made of rough
      and scratchy animal hair. Broadcloth is a densely woven,
      smooth fabric, no longer much used in contemporary
      clothing.

51   *Every time I come out here it looks like Playland!*: an amusement
      park.

51   *roué*: French for what used to be called a 'rake', a playboy.

56   *Zeppelin*: a Zeppelin was a dirigible, an airship used in the
      1930s. In America they can still be seen flying as novelties
      (not as transportation) and are sometimes called 'blimps'.

64   *Mahatma Gandhi*: (1869–1948) the pre-eminent political
      and spiritual leader of India during the struggle for
      Indian independence. He employed tactics of non-violent
      resistance and civil disobedience. He led a simple,
      abstemious life and was very thin, hence Chris's joke.

66   *No, he was always one year ahead of the draft*: in 1940 (still
      peacetime in the US) the government instituted a system
      of compulsory, one-year military service for men between
      the ages of twenty-one and thirty-five. After Pearl Harbor,
      when the US entered the war, the draft law was amended,
      eliminating the exemptions (married men, etc.). All men
      between twenty and forty-five became eligible for the
      draft. Ultimately more than ten million men were drafted
      in the Second World War.

67   *Eagle Scouts the three of you*: Eagle Scout is the top rank in
      the Boy Scouts of America, a nationwide club subscribing
      to high moral principles.

67   *Andy Gump*: Andy Gump was a popular cartoon-strip
      character in several national and local newspapers.

Questions for Further Study

1 Consider the significance of the play's title.
2 Compare and contrast Joe Keller to Miller's most famous character, Willy Loman in *Death of a Salesman*: Do they share values? How are each man's values tested? Are their suicides similarly motivated?
3 What symbolic elements illuminate the meaning of the play?
4 Some readers/spectators have found Larry's letter, whipped out at the last minute, too contrived as a plot device. Argue for or against its timing and its dramatic necessity.
5 What is the effect of the play taking place in the Kellers' back yard? Consider the importance of neighbourhood.
6 What can be deduced about mid-twentieth-century American society from this play? What evidence supports your ideas? Consider the spectrum of attitudes articulated by the characters, ranging from optimism to cynicism.
7 *All My Sons* is, like O'Neill's most famous play, also a 'long day's journey into night'; how does the morning-to-night time-scheme function as a way of understanding the play's vision?
8 We see four couples in the play: what does Miller seem to be saying about the institution of marriage?
9 'Denial', a self-protective psychological device for hiding an unpleasant truth from oneself, is prevalent among these characters. Why do they need to persist in denial?
10 What is the symbolic significance of Chris's name as it affects the dynamica of the plays?
11 To what extent is *All My Sons* an anti-war play?
12 Bert's role is small, although significant. What does Miller reveal by Bert's appearance in Act One?
13 *All My Sons*, it could be argued, is Miller's only completely realistic play. Miller seems to adhere to the conventions of

realism, especially that of the 'fourth wall'; discuss the necessity of naturalism for the impact of this play in performance.

14 The elaborate set directions indicate how important it was to Miller to create a very specific world: which elements of the set directions seem crucial and why?

15 What do you understand 'ensemble' to mean? Should the cast create the sense of an ensemble to indicate family or neighbourhood?

16 Do you think the confrontation between Joe and Chris should be a physical fight? Different choices are made by different directors.

17 The lighting design needs to create visual clues for the audience to indicate that time has passed, but it can also create an emotional atmosphere. How do you imagine this evocation?

18 Imagine you are the casting director: describe the central qualities you are looking for in the four major roles. Although accomplished actors can transcend physical attributes, nevertheless audiences tend to 'read' a character through the actor. How might this affect the play?

19 How crucial is it that the play be located by costuming, etc. in mid-twentieth-century America? Can you imagine this play successfully relocated to another time and place to make a similar sociopolitical statement?

20 George's entrance is postponed as he waits in the car offstage; what is the effect of this delay? What does it tell the audience about the approaching climax? Like many plays, *All My Sons* is built on entrances and exits. Consider the timing of the comings and goings. How does this work, for example, in the conclusion?

21 Sophoclean irony depends on the audience knowing more than the character does, so that it is not the revelation of the secret but the character's reaction to the secret that we wait for. Analyse the way Miller has built his play on this classical device.

TOBY ZINMAN is Professor of English at the University of the Arts in Philadelphia, where she was awarded the prize for Distinguished Teaching. She has lectured internationally on contemporary American drama, including a semester as Fulbright professor in Israel and another as a visiting lecturer in China. Her third book, *Edward Albee*, was published in 2008. She is also the theatre critic for Philadelphia's major daily newspaper, *The Inquirer*, and a frequent contributor to a variety of arts magazines.

ENOCH BRATER is the Kenneth T. Rowe Collegiate Professor of Dramatic Literature at the University of Michigan. He has published widely in the field of modern drama, and is an internationally renowned expert on such figures as Samuel Beckett and Arthur Miller. His recent books include *Arthur Miller: A Playwright's Life and Works*, *Arthur Miller's America: Theater and Culture in a Time of Change*, and *Arthur Miller's Global Theater: How an American Playwright Is Performed on Stages around the World*.